Praise for *Understorey*

'A beautiful, quiet, achingly tender book. A year spent with weeds; giving voice to the exquisite and the everyday alike… It's a reminder that the circle always turns; the light always comes back' **Kerri ní Dochartaigh, author of *Thin Places***

'This tranquil, meditative book is all about the quiet pleasure of examining something closely in order to truly appreciate it' *Daily Mail*

'This thoughtful and beautifully written book is a balm to the soul. Structured as a calendar year spent looking at wildflowers in the author's neighbourhood, and sketching them as part of an attempt to slow down and observe more carefully, this book is part illustrated artist's diary, and part meditation on the process of drawing: what it means to look, take time to observe, and to attempt to record what we see on the page. I drank it all in and it has changed me forever' **Vicky MacKenzie, author of *For Thy Great Pain Have Mercy On My Little Pain***

'Anna Chapman Parker weaves together art history, botany, ecosystems, and the routines of everyday life in this gracefully illuminating account of a year drawing weeds. Through the shifting seasons, Chapman Parker's drawings and prose reveal the extraordinary value of plants that are generally taken for granted, ignored, or obliterated, and the power of stopping to look carefully, pen in hand' **Alixe Bovey, Dean and Deputy Director at The Courtauld**

'A delicately written study of the joys and difficulties of paying attention' **Jessie Greengrass, author of *The High House***

'Anna Chapman Parker approaches the struggle to find creative fulfilment in a world full of distraction with the same generosity she extends to some of our most overlooked and downtrodden urban flora. This book is as clear-eyed as it is beautiful' **Florence Wilkinson, author of *Wild City***

'What a brilliant idea, to fit into the interstices of days full of work and two children, the very plants that are themselves so good at filling the interstices of our daily lives. The attention that Anna Chapman Parker has given to the ordinary weeds surrounding her, both in drawings and words, gives them a heightened glamour, presence and worth' **Ruth Pavey, author of *A Wood of One's Own***

'A year of sketching and musing on the unplanted, unplanned, unremarkable greenery that surrounds us all every day. A celebration of disorder and doing nothing – the perfect antidote to the modern belief that something only exists once it's been captured by your phone' **Ken Thompson, author of *Common or Garden***

UNDERSTOREY
A Year Among Weeds

Anna Chapman Parker

DUCKWORTH

First published in the United Kingdom by Duckworth in 2024

This paperback edition published by Duckworth in 2025

Duckworth, an imprint of Duckworth Books Ltd
1 Golden Court, Richmond, TW9 1EU, United Kingdom
www.duckworthbooks.co.uk

Copyright © Anna Chapman Parker, 2024

All rights reserved. No part of this publication may be reproduced, stored in a retrieval system, or transmitted, in any form or by any means electronic, mechanical, photocopying, recording or otherwise, without the prior permission of the publisher.

The right of Anna Chapman Parker to be identified as the Author of this Work has been asserted by her in accordance with the Copyright, Designs and Patents Act 1988.

A catalogue record for this book is available from the British Library

Book design by Danny Lyle

Printed and bound in Great Britain by Clays Ltd, Elcograf S.p.A.

The authorised representative in the EEA is Easy Access System Europe, Mustamäe tee 50, 10621 Tallinn, Estonia.

Paperback ISBN: 9780715655689
eISBN: 9780715655214

To Martin, Frida, Marlowe and Dash, who put up with all the lagging behind.

… patterns of attention – what we choose to notice and what we do not – are how we render reality for ourselves, and thus have a direct bearing on what we feel is possible at any given time

Jenny Odell, *How to Do Nothing: Resisting the Attention Economy*, 2019

It is not only what you actually see along the path, but what you remember to have seen, that gives it its beauty.

Richard Jefferies, *Nature Near London*, 1883

DRAWINGS & OTHER ARTWORKS

BEFORE
Piero della Francesca, *The Baptism of Christ*, 1437 — xvii

JANUARY
perennial ryegrass (*Lolium perenne*) — 5
ivy (*Hedera helix*) — 9
cow parsley (*Anthriscus sylvestris*) — 12
cleavers (*Galium aparine*) — 15
creeping thistle (*Cirsium arvense*) — 17
Karl Blossfeldt, *Dandelion*, 1928 — **20**
bramble (*Rubus fruticosus*) — 23

FEBRUARY
cleavers (*Galium aparine*) — 26
barley (*Hordeum vulgare*) — 31
hart's tongue fern (*Asplenium scolopendrium*) — 33
snowdrops (*Galanthus nivalis*) — 34
grassy bank — 36
dandelions (*Taraxacum officinale*) — 38
Anna Atkins, *Dandelion*, c.1854 — **41**

MARCH
nettles (*Urtica dioica*) — 45
alkanet (*Pentaglottis sempervirens*) — 48
periwinkles (*Vinca minor*) — 52
Giovanni di Paolo, *Paradise*, 1445 — **55**

spotted deadnettle (*Lamium maculatum*)	56
lesser celandine (*Ficaria verna*)	59
curly dock (*Rumex crispus*)	61
creeping buttercup (*Ranunculus repens*)	62

APRIL

daisies (*Bellis perennis*)	69
Richard Long, *England 1968*, 1968	**72**
honesty (*Lunaria annua*)	75
ground ivy (*Glechoma hederacea*)	80
scurvy-grass (*Cochlearia officinalis*)	85
three-cornered leek (*Allium triquetrum*)	86
wild garlic (*Allium ursinum*)	89

MAY

groundsel (*Senecio vulgaris*)	91
mouse-ear chickweed (*Cerastium vulgatum*)	96
greater stitchwort (*Rabelera holostea*)	98
ribwort plantain (*Plantago lanceolata*)	107
bluebell (*Hyacinthoides non-scripta*)	109
Spanish bluebell (*Hyacinthoides hispanica*)	109
Selfheal, from the *Circa Instans* (Egerton 747), *c*.1300	**102**

JUNE

cow parsley (*Anthriscus sylvestris*)	121
slender speedwell (*Veronica filiformis*)	122
sowthistle (*Sonchus* spp.)	126
Bramble, from the *Vienna Dioscorides*, *c*.512	**128**
forget-me-not (*Myosotis sylvatica*)	133
annual meadow grass (*Poa* spp.)	136

JULY

self-heal (*Prunella vulgaris*)	139
curly dock (*Rumex crispus*)	142
nettle-leaved bellflower (*Campanula trachelium*)	145
buttercups (*Ranunculus* spp.)	147
perennial sowthistle (*Sonchus Arvensis*)	148
spear thistle (*Cirsium vulgare*)	150
knapweed (*Centaurea nigra*)	153
Dorothy Cross, *Foxgloves*, 2007–2021	**157**

AUGUST

rosebay willowherb (*Chamerion angustifolium*)	166
João Penalva, *Caryatia Japonica*, from *Addressing the Weeds in Hiroshima*, 1997	**168**
Dima Tolkachov, *New Weeds*, 2022	**170**
herb Robert (*Geranium robertianum*)	173
meadow cranesbill (*Geranium pratense*)	177
mayweed (*Matricaria chamomilla*)	178
dandelion (*Taraxacum* spp.)	181
yarrow (*Achillea millefolium*)	185

SEPTEMBER

meadow with ox-eye daisies (*Leucanthemum vulgare*)	189
comfrey (*Symphytum officinale*)	193
campion seedheads (*Silene dioica*)	195
ragwort (*Jacobaea vulgaris*)	197
Albrecht Dürer, *Great Piece of Turf*, 1503	**198**
hairy bittercress (*Cardamine hirsuta*)	204
weeds in lawn	207

OCTOBER

honesty seedheads (*Lunaria annua*)	209
purple toadflax (*Linaria purpurea*)	212
white deadnettle (*Lamium album*)	215
shepherd's purse (*Capsella bursa-pastoris*)	216
Sunday morning	218
Maria Thereza Alves, *Seeds of Change:*	
***A Floating Ballast Seed Garden* (Bristol), 2012–2016**	**223**
broom (*Cytisus scoparius*)	224

NOVEMBER

mugwort (*Artemisia vulgaris*)	228
mallow (*Malva sylvestris*)	231
teasel (*Dipsacus fullonum*)	232
ragwort (*Jacobaea vulgaris*)	237
cow parsley, new shoot (*Anthriscus sylvestris*)	240
Simryn Gill, *Vegetation 3*, 1999	**242**
cleavers (*Galium aparine*)	244
pellitory-of-the-wall (*Parietaria judaica*)	247

DECEMBER

grasses	252
Precious Okoyomon, *Earthseed*, 2020	**257**
nettles (*Urtica dioica*)	258
at the edge of the carpark	261
sowthistle (*Sonchus* spp.)	262
wood avens, new shoot (*Geum urbanum*)	267
grasses in a ditch	268
hogweed (*Heracleum sphondylium*)	272

POSTSCRIPT

The Wilton Diptych, c.1395–1399 [detail]	276

LIST OF PLANTS ENCOUNTERED

spp.= several species

alkanet *Pentaglottis sempervirens*
barren strawberry *Potentilla sterilis*
bindweed *Convolvulus* spp.
bittercress, hairy *Cardamine hirsuta*
black horehound *Ballota nigra*
black medick *Medicago lupulina*
bluebell, Spanish *Hyacinthoides hispanica*
bluebell, English *Hyacinthoides non-scripta*
bramble *Rubus* spp.
broom *Cytisus scoparius*
burdock, lesser *Arctium minus*
campion, bladder *Silene vulgaris*
campion, red *Silene dioica*
celandine, lesser *Ficaria verna*
chickweed *Stellaria media*
cleavers (stickyweed) *Galium aparine*
clover, red *Trifolium pratense*
clover, white *Trifolium repens*
coltsfoot *Tussilago farara*
comfrey *Symphytum officinale*
cow parsley *Anthriscus sylvestris*
cranesbill, meadow *Geranium pratense*
cranesbill, hedgerow *Geranium pyrenaicum*
climbing corydalis *Ceratocapnos claviculata*
daisy, common *Bellis perennis*
dandelion *Taraxacum* spp.
dock, broad-leaved *Rumex obtusifolius*

dock, curly *Rumex crispus*
feverfew *Tanacetum parthenium*
forget-me-not *Myosotis* spp.
foxglove *Digitalis purpurea*
fumitory (earthsmoke) *Fumaria officinalis*
garlic mustard *Alliaria petiolata*
grass, annual meadow *Poa annua*
grass, perennial rye- *Lolium perenne*
greater stitchwort *Rabelera holostea*
ground ivy *Glechoma hederacea*
groundsel *Senecio vulgaris*
harebell *Campanula rotundifolia*
hart's tongue fern *Asplenium scolopendrium*
hawkweed *Hieracium* spp.
herb Robert *Geranium robertianum*
himalayan balsam *Impatiens glandulifera*
hoary mustard *Hirschfeldia incana*
hogweed, common *Heracleum sphondylium*
honesty *Lunaria annua*
ivy *Hedera* spp.
ivy-leaved toadflax *Cymbalaria muralis*
knapweed *Centaurea nigra*
mallow *Malva sylvestris*
mayweed *Tripleurospermum* spp.
mouse-ear chickweed *Cerastium* spp.
mugwort *Artemisia vulgaris*
nettle, stinging *Urtica dioica*
nettle-leaved bellflower *Campanula trachelium*
nipplewort *Lapsana communis*
ox-eye daisy *Leucanthemum vulgare*

pellitory-of-the-wall *Parietaria judaica*
periwinkles *Vinca minor*
pineapple weed *Matricaria discoidea*
plantain, broad-leaved *Plantago major*
plantain, ribwort *Plantago lanceolata*
poppy, Welsh *Papaver cambricum*
petty spurge *Euphorbia peplus*
purple toadflax *Linaria purpurea*
ragwort *Jacobaea vulgaris* syn. *Senecio jacobaea*
red valerian *Centranthus ruber*
scabious, field *Knautia arvensis*
scurvy-grass *Cochlearia officinalis*
self-heal *Prunella vulgaris*
shepherd's purse *Capsella bursa-pastoris*
silverweed *Potentilla anserina*
sneezewort *Achillea ptarmica*
snowdrop, common *Galanthus nivalis*
sowthistle, annual or perennial *Sonchus* spp.
speedwell *Veronica* spp.
tansy *Tanacetum vulgare*
tare, hairy *Vicia hirsuta*
teasel *Dipsacus fullonum*
thale cress *Arabidopsis thaliana*
thistle, creeping *Cirsium arvense*
thistle, spike/spear *Cirsium vulgare*
three-cornered leek/garlic *Allium triquetrum*
vetch, common *Vicia sativa*
violet, dog *Viola riviniana*
violet, sweet *Viola odorata*
white deadnettle *Lamium album*

wild garlic (ramsons) *Allium ursinum*
willowherb, hoary *Epilobium parviflorum*
willowherb, rosebay *Chamerion angustifolium*
wood avens (herb bennet) *Geum urbanum*
wood-sorrel *Oxalis acetosella*
yarrow *Achillea millefolium*

BEFORE

I'm sitting on an old carrier bag, perched on a heap of hardened earth at the back of the house. November. A vegetable patch started in a more optimistic month has run amok. Something flowering into post-it note yellow has taken over the nearest corner. Charlock or wild mustard maybe, the seeds blown in on the wind or excreted by a bird. Stillness seems to resonate in the air, palpable after a flurry of activity: my children have left for school and the commuter traffic has fallen away; I imagine across town a thousand exhalations into office chairs.

I began drawing here yesterday but was stopped by rain and a call from the house. I've come back with the same pen and notebook, pretty much the same viewpoint, eyes, musculature and grip – but today my quality and pace of movements is different, and that comes out in the drawing. A drawing is symptomatic. Its lines emerge speaking of infinitesimal tensions, softnesses and uncertainties, themselves produced by currents of mood and feeling that might otherwise have gone unnoticed. The lines can lead you back from what you're seeing, back into your body.

The rooks are cawing overhead. A nearby blackbird makes small hopeful movements like rustling litter. I've not got much down and none of my lines are tethered to the ground, but I need to get back inside to my own desk. I stand up and shake a numb leg, look down at the drawing from the height I am: it seems enough.

It began as a way of drawing nothing – as near as I could get to that. I always had a notebook and a pen in my bag. My children were very young, I was rarely alone, and felt an urgent need to find a still and focused space of my own, however briefly. We'd head out and there would be some hiatus when I wasn't needed and I'd grab my chance. No time to think about it or search around for a subject – just drop down and draw whatever was growing through the ground. The early years of motherhood, when so much internal dialogue is replaced by speaking and attending to another, can effect a kind of erasure; the deepest voice in the mind's mix placed on mute. Those early drawings were often little more than a few lines scratched out during my children's brief intervals of play, but they became an important record for me of my continuing agency and identity, independent of work and care.

The drawings became more sustained as my children grew, sometimes done alone, or with barely a glance at my increasingly independent companions. Beyond a vague curiosity, though, the plants still didn't mean much to me; I recognised very few by name, and that was a relief. My lack of knowledge precluded any sense of having to care about them. They were simply something to latch on to, pulling me from myself and out on to the page. My sketchbook became a kind of room of my own, peopled with an assortment of weedy inhabitants I didn't have to talk to.

The shift began with a six-hundred-year-old bindweed. On a day in London, I'd wandered into the National Gallery, and,

Piero della Francesca, *The Baptism of Christ*, 1437 [detail]
egg tempera on poplar, 167 x 116cm
National Gallery, London

finding myself in the galleries of early Italian paintings, among the glowing, gilded rows, cerulean blue, dark umber, venetian red, I realised I was looking at the ground in the paintings more than at the figures. The plants were everywhere – dotted all over the dry ochre earth, emerging from the cracks in every rock, creeping out, even, from the edges of the picture frames. Piero della Francesca, *The Baptism of Christ*, 1437: I didn't know the story, but here at the protagonists' feet was a cluster of weeds as intimately familiar as my own hand. They were lightly and deftly drawn, picked out in olive green: grasses, some vague wispy flowers, and the heart-shaped leaves of the bindweed at the end of my own street.

It was this encounter with painted weeds, the same flora I knew, observed half a millennium ago, which marked the beginning of a new way of relating to the plants. Weeds were no longer accidental green stuff that didn't matter: they were a living constancy, a kind of wild connective tissue across time and place. I wanted to know them better. What were these plants that accompany every walk outside, yet pass beneath our notice? When and how did they emerge, flower, subside and disappear through the course of a year? And what constituted a weed, anyway?

Most importantly, could I get to know these often disregarded plants via the experience of looking – that still, concentrated presence that I encountered in the museum's paintings, and experienced myself when drawing? Could my research occur, like my opportunistic and happenstance drawings, through coming across what was there rather than through a pre-ordained plan? And could I make a written account of looking as it happened, without my words marking a separate, desk-based *afterwards*?

This book is my attempt at approaching these questions. I set out very simply to observe and record the plants I found over the course of a year, using drawings and words, and doing the observing in the places they grew, not in a studio, later. All the drawing and initial writing took place along weed-lined pavements, carpark edges, parks, footpaths and roadside verges near my home. I live in a small town in the north of England, not a rural idyll; you could find most of the plants I've recorded within a short walk of almost any front door.

As I went out and looked at them, the plants linked me to other eyes looking at the same shapes across the centuries, like Piero's bindweed; illustrations in medieval manuscripts, early photographic experiments, more recent and contemporary artworks too. I have included some of these images and observations alongside my own.

I began this book with the intention of studying weeds. But as my notes and drawings accumulated I realised that as much as I was learning about the plants themselves, I was learning more about how to encounter them; how I might attend to those encounters. As John Berger observed after making some drawings of a friend, 'Maybe [they] are not proper drawings but simply sketch maps of an encounter. Maps that may make it less likely to get lost. A question of hope.'[1]

JANUARY

> What do we do when we do nothing, what do
> we hear when we hear nothing,
> what happens when nothing happens?
>
> Paul Virilio, describing his work with Georges Perec on
> the journal *Cause Commune*[2]

If I'm going to draw a category of things defined by their unwantedness, I might as well begin at the leanest point of the year, when there is least to attract the eye. As I walk through the streets of the town where I live, up past the shops and through the park down to the river, very few flowers quake the air: the odd white deadnettle, grubby in the verge, a handful of sowthistles bordering the bins, and down at the water's edge the acid-yellow gorse, which never gives up.* Only litter lights up the municipal paths. Colour seems to have drained even from the greens that still stand; at the edge of the carpark nettles have wizened to wire, overgrown grasses collapse in sullen heaps, the early teeth of dandelions cling to the tarmac. A sense of stilled

---

* Hence the saying, 'When gorse is out of bloom, kissing is out of fashion.'

growth pervades; where there's profusion it seems to smack of waste, of matter to be cleared away. On the path beyond the station, where in summer the grasses and wildflowers grow tall enough to hide in, a succession of storms and frosts has battered it all back to the quick.

Along the council paths and playparks the grass is in stasis now, and won't need cutting for weeks more. Grass in winter can feel like the absence of anything else. This is green at its most unremarkable, green that's just there, reading less as living vegetation than a default mode for ground. Easy to forget that there are individual plants making up this buff-green plane, strewn here and there with twigs of ash. I realise I don't even know what the stuff is, and pull up a fistful of stems to identify later.* Sycamore leaves scurry past, quick as mice.

The grass here is a deliberate, municipal choice, and maintained as such. But its edges grow threadbare like patches of worn clothing rubbed thin by the body's friction. As the path narrows and pedestrians step aside to let each another pass, patches of it are trampled down to mud, a kind of violence wrought by politeness. And now the weeds break through: low zingy spumes of cleavers beginning; straggling attempts at pellitory-of-the-wall. A hard grey rosette of thistle, grimly decorative; a corduroy leaf of plantain.

Unwanted man-made things collect in the edges, too, a tidemark of sorts. Bottle tops and aluminium ring-pulls; the plastic wrappers of small sweet comforts; cigarette stubs (fewer now), pocket spillages, drifts of grit.

---

* Most likely perennial ryegrass (*Lolium perenne*).

JANUARY

I stand listing it all into my phone, my jaw half-numb with cold, recording things barely more lively than my own breath. 'What happens when nothing happens?' Georges Perec asked himself, looking at the page, the bed, the room, the street, the city in which he found himself.[3] How do we occupy such spaces when nothing in particular is going on? Can describing what surrounds us, in the careful, exhaustive detail of its mundanity, form a sense of being there – or does our use of language always take us somewhere else?

Like the everyday things that Perec observed, encountered largely without note, weeds are everywhere and nowhere at the same time. In my town, as in any other, they're arriving at any given moment by seed on the wind, by stolons and tubers tunnelling underground, via excretions of birds, dogs, insects, human spit. They are borne clinging to passing sleeves, embedded in the turn-ups of trousers, in pocket seams, the treads of soles, the feet of birds. They land and root in the *terrain vague* of the traffic island, building site or carpark edge, in the unusable gap behind bin or bench. They thrive in cracks in paving, in dirt collecting round lamp-posts, bins and gutters. Their places are the edge-zones where one kind of utility awkwardly meets another. Their green marks out the spaces we can't use – else they'd be removed. Only in the most affluent streets do weeds find no foothold.

What is a weed? The usual definitions tend to say more about the speaker than their object. Though efforts have been made over the centuries to categorise weeds by their behaviours, weeds don't exist as any kind of botanical group. A weed is much more of an opinion, a reflection of social and cultural behaviour, than a vegetal type. ('Plants become weeds when they obstruct our plans,' as Richard Mabey has observed.) The English word is derived from the Old Saxon *wiod*, itself related to the Old High German *wiota* meaning fern, a plant that is wild and prolific. These two adjectives describe the essential characteristics of weeds as most of us would understand them: they are plants that come up without being cultivated, and that multiply abundantly, often in a way that's not easy to control. Their proliferation, which often leads to the epithet 'invasive', is explained by another quality of weeds: their ability to grow in many different habitats. A weed is a plant that is wild, prolific and adaptable. That is the guiding definition I'll use for the plants I'll write about here.*

This hummock of grass coming up between the paving – growing here as weed, 'a plant out of place' as the saying goes – is as good a place as any to begin. *What do we see when we see 'nothing'?* Crouched on the edge of the path, I get out my sketchbook, pen, fumble with a bottle of ink. Almost immediately my body makes as if to turn away. Moving through the resistance to looking is like pushing through water. I see a clod of greenish stalks, messy, irregular, nondescript, the size of a man's hand. Letting in the information involves some recalibration, a lowering of the threshold of interest, to ask, *what does this turfy mass require of me? How can I register it onto paper?*

---

* In other European languages the word for weed is more explicitly negative: French and Spanish have *mauvaise herbe* and *mala hierba*, 'bad plants', and Italian uses the pejorative suffix *-accia* to make *erbaccia*, a herb that's nasty, ugly or cursed. In German a weed is an *unkraut* or 'un-herb', not a real plant. So while 'weed' does carry negative connotations, linguistically it's relatively neutral. I'm grateful to Nina Edwards' book *Weeds* (London: Reaktion, 2015) for these etymological descriptions.

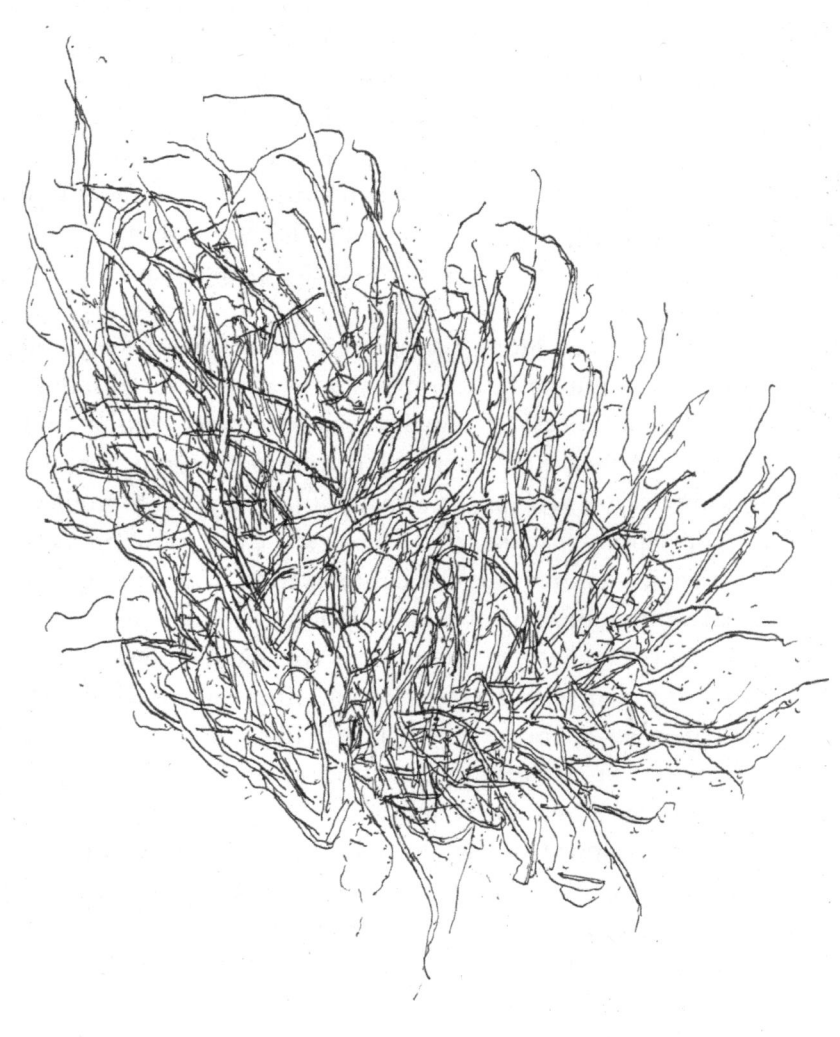

2 January: perennial ryegrass (*Lolium perenne*)

After the first instant of sight, the mind latches on to words, first naming, then falling upon description in the way a young child might reach for a toy. The mind can't sit empty-handed, after all. Perhaps its narration is jumbled, perhaps it grows more articulate. Well, good – but is this the same as looking, or am I now doing something else: describing? Can we look in any kind of sustained way without collapsing back into language? I wedge my bottle of ink between two concrete slabs, dip my pen into the gloopy black.

Drawing is at once a gesture at its most simple – making a mark – and at its most impossible – a move to reproduce reality. This process of remaining in one place, fixing your sight on an object in front of you and marking its outlines as accurately as you can on a sheet of paper, poses a problem which, happily, can never be resolved. Even with frequent practice it requires all the concentration you can muster to enact the innumerable calculations between light, eye and hand. It takes an openness to continually changing or correcting yourself as you add new lines to the marks on the paper, an openness which is less like patiently listening and more like actively interrupting yourself reading a live newsfeed by refreshing it several times a sentence (at times you're too gripped in the story to reload the page but now you're reading old news, for the updates are coming at every instant). And it requires a sustained period of time – a few minutes at least – to get something vaguely recognisable down on paper.

Sometimes this may be enough to quieten the mind's monologue for brief moments. I don't pretend there is anything pure about it. The words don't cease, but there can be a sense, at least for odd instants, that the looking is occurring without them.*

The writer Annie Dillard described a similar loosening of experience from language when, in Virginia's Blue Ridge Mountains in 1974, she watched a muskrat foraging in the creek at dusk.

> In the forty minutes I watched him, he never saw me, smelled me, or heard me at all [...] I never knew I was there, either. For that forty minutes last night I was as purely sensitive and mute as a photographic plate; I received impressions, but I did not print out captions. My own self-awareness had disappeared [...]⁴

Dillard's account evokes the immersive, highly focused mental state sometimes referred to as *flow*, a state which tends to involve a suspension of our awareness of both self and time passing.** It's a feeling which might also be described as being everywhere and nowhere at the same time.

3 January
Walking home from the station, I pass a group of desiccated ragwort stems by the side of the road. The papery stalks are

---

* I have experimented with attempting to verbalise the visual calculating I'm doing when drawing by recording myself drawing 'out loud' – vocalising what I'm following with my eye, what's registering, what micro-decisions my pen is making as quickly as I can catch them. The result is a series of incredibly boring half-sentences, contradictions, grunts; mostly meaningless combinations of prepositions.

** Flow states were identified and named by the psychologist Mihály Csíkszentmihályi in 1975.

still hanging on, far more resilient than they look. Everywhere I turn, new lines are revealing themselves as the year loses more and more of its fat. Pellitory-of-the-wall, foliage tattered black by the last frost, discloses its clinging structure. Brambles' thorn-studded arcs have fewer leaves to interrupt their shape. The nettles are reduced to drunken, hirsute verticals. Even the evergreens are leggier, strands of ivy becoming gappy, showing their gripping aerial roots. The plants are going backwards in the drawing of themselves, back to the first downward line. Their loss of foliage reveals the vulnerabilities of survival.

Heading back through town now. Christmas tree needles pepper the gutters.

6 January

The street ahead is clean, a picture turned monochrome. Nothing coming through the seams where wall becomes pavement, or behind the gutters, the favoured damp places, or even in the neglected corners at the back of the bins. No green here at all. But beneath the street, invisibly, improbably, so much is happening. Seeds are biding their time. Some of them perhaps lodged beneath the tarmac decades ago, yet are still able to germinate given as slight a chance as a sliver of light through a new crack, the spread of damp or a leak from a pipe. Others, seeded here only weeks ago, are beginning the acceleration of cell division that will stretch a shoot upward into visibility with its first embryonic leaves.

Along the edge of the river path which skirts one side of town, there's a seam of new green where the river silt has caught in the crack between asphalt and stone edge. *Galium aparine*, cleavers or stickyweed, beginning as bright, verdant froth, delineate the

6 January: ivy (*Hedera helix*)

contours of the path. Weeds mark the history of man-made constructions like this, but perhaps above all their frailties: the weak spots, joins and repairs. Small failures and misjudgements are highlighted green within weeks. And absences too: a door's threshold furring over with moss when the occupants move out, a front garden erupting into willowherb when its owner injures his back.

The first plant to catch my drawing eye here is a woody nightshade (*Solanum dulcamara*) I've passed many times before. Each berry drops from its stem accompanied by a droplet of water: a double globe. (If I stay to draw the nightshade, will I draw the droplet as well? Is this part of the plant right now?) But my feet have moved me on – it's in deep shade, too cold to stop. The next stretch of bank faces south. I know there will be ivy here in full sun. I can draw with my back baked in its warmth and have long enough to work before my fingers numb.

The ivy here (*Hedera* sp.) rampages up a bank as tall as a house. It's covered in berries – some of the fruits pinkish brown and black, the smaller ones still lime-yellow and tender. Held in spheres of radiating stalks, the berries are as ornamental as something medieval worked in enamel. But the new foliage is yellowish, and plasticky. I flatten a smooth-veined shape between my hands. This is an old plant and its leaves no longer bear the typical three lobes but have rounded out in their maturity, becoming curled hearts.

It's more than sun that makes me want to stop here. It's the light reflecting off the leaves, a watery gleam. No wonder ivy dominates the rituals of deep winter, its gloss bringing reflected light to the shadiest depths. What clearer symbol of continuity and endurance than a steadfast, clinging evergreen? An emblem of protection for millennia, guarding the imagination variously from intoxication, witches, disease in cattle.

The ancient Greeks garlanded their poets with ivy crowns; Celtic pagans used it in solstice rites; now we decorate our doors with Christmas wreaths. I snap a length off quite easily, curl it around itself into a hoop. The stalks seem to want to give way, to accommodate any curve with ease just as they encircle trunks of trees or the contours of a bank. Their curling linearity makes the vines an ideal form of decoration for the edges of things, too, where they can run on and on with no need to terminate. Across the centuries, miles and miles of ivy, along with other scandent vines, have bordered the pages of illuminated manuscripts.*

Ivy is vilified for threatening the trees that host it, but in fact it is not at all parasitic; it can creep over ground as well as tree trunk, and makes its own nutrients. Most trees are unharmed by ivy unless it reaches the highest branches and begins to bush out, making the crown top-heavy. In the meantime, ivy provides an exceptionally rich habitat for wildlife, supporting at least fifty insect species and offering valuable winter nectar and pollen for bees.

A beetle lands on the stem I'm drawing, too quick to note down, then leaps to my page. Do I include the beetle? Does acknowledging its journey across my paper break some papery fourth wall? My nib hovers, then returns to tracing the stem, finding the joint where a lower flower stalk makes its exit.

One certainty: it has no perfect circle or straight line. No rushing green vertical is as effortless as it seems at arm's length.

---

* See for example the lines of ivy, trefoils and vine leaves in the *Luttrell Psalter*, c.1300.

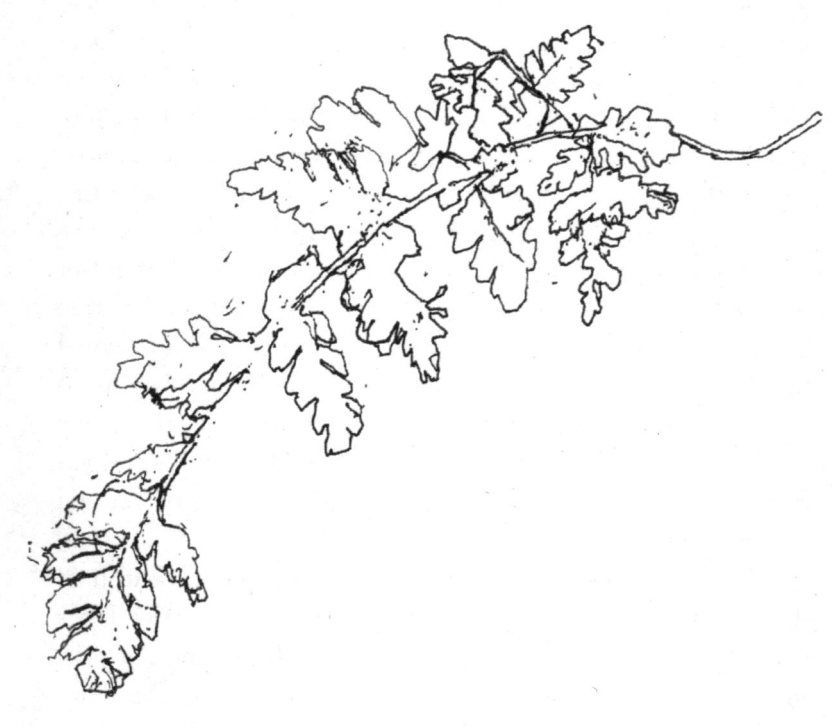

8 January: cow parsley (*Anthriscus sylvestris*)

No berry is exactly spherical. The eye reports in shorthand even at close range. To look past each abbreviated shape to find its complexity, the places where it departs from known geometry or expected profile, requires an ongoing effort at assuming nothing.

I start for home. Pass the nightshade again; the droplets have gone. A drawing made in the time taken to evaporate the dew.

7 January
A week into the year, and following the weeds, I'm finding myself eyeing the ground each time I leave the house, scanning the pavements even if I'm only heading to the car across the street. It has become a reflex already, this slanting look. Most days I'll walk the dog, and once school resumes so will the daily trip to take my children there and back, a walk that brings us either through the town, or up the street and round the edges of a park and recreation ground. Despite the fact that I work from home, all this ensures I'll still find time each day to check on what is happening: what plants are coming through, what's flowering, what's budding up or blowing seed or dying back. And when I can't make time to stop and draw I can at least make note of what is happening as I walk. My phone is filling up with voice memos and blurry videos of plants to look up back at my desk. At weekends and when work allows I'll travel further out of town, but for the most part I want my search to occupy the interstitial intervals of a working day, just as the weeds find their scant chance in cracks between the paving slabs and other fixed necessities of the street.

Too cold to draw today – not for me in my padded coat but for my poor patient hound, who whines, flanks trembling, at every stop. I make do with noting the sequence of characters along the pavement edge, learning their names by marking them out under my breath as I head up to the shops. A weedy, gap-toothed list: *groundsel, shepherd's purse, dock, hawkweed, cleavers.* The rhythm of their iterance becomes an incantation of presence. Dense spirals of ragworts are emerging through the grass, there's something gritted-teeth about them; on the wall a wild campanula is toughing it out beside the tiny succulent called stonecrop. Chickweed is budding up: soon I'll be able to look for its tiny white stars.

8 January
Early morning by the river. Walking the dog, I realise I'm starting to check in on certain plants like nodding acquaintances – fellow inmates, even. Here in the cleft of two capstones is a patch of ivy-leaved toadflax that I first noticed last summer. No flowers now, but the leaves have fattened up, a bold-type version of last year's script, raised up by an undergrowth of fresh emerald.

It's more than a fortnight since the winter solstice, but in plant time the climb back up toward the light doesn't seem to have begun. Everything is still falling away; even the ivy droops, and below it the greenery of the verge looks barely vegetal. I can't isolate in those tangled shrouds of nettles what was stem, leaf, flower, nor can I feel bothered to. The only hues to catch the eye are the felt-tip reds and blues of crumpled litter. I'm scanning the path ahead for relief, mood as deflated as those discarded crisp packets.

On this day in 1884 in Sussex, the English nature writer Richard Jefferies wrote in his diary:

16 January: cleavers (*Galium aparine*)

> [I] never go for a walk in the fields without seeing one thing at least however small to give me hope, the frond of a fern among dead leaves.[5]

One thing however small. The need to look more modestly. Unfashionable word. The lines of the grasses, how they interrupt each other, a kind of silent chatter.

A few paces further – droplets of rain caught perfectly in the curves of new dandelion leaves. The rosette of a new mallow appearing, its leaves still concertinaed tight, emerging with mute intensity.

I check in on a dead ragwort I've been keeping an eye on. Still there, bleached to bone. An image of forbearance.

12 January
Fresh growths of cleavers sparkling against the sodden-dark leaf-fall.

16 January
It's bitterly cold, and I've come out in the wrong coat (optimism of the first sunshine in a while). On my way back from the shops I crouch midway down a bank of steps to draw new cleavers emerging in the verge.

I follow the angles of each stalk and leaf as obediently and accurately as I can. A sense of loyalty about it, like a dog clinging to the side of its owner, alert to her every move. The slightest deviation of a line will change its character – now a jauntier stem, now a more downcast turn of leaf. But looking at a plant is rarely about the facts we record. It's much messier, and I want to reflect that complication in the drawing. Not just

25 January: creeping thistle (*Cirsium arvense*)

to note *the stem goes from here to there, branches into five leaflets at equal intervals*, but the awkward, convoluted experience of it. Does that mean including the shadow of my hair that's falling across the page, intersecting with a stem? Or letting the song lyric or conversation running through my head leak out of the pen? It's something of this I'm trying to follow, in shape and line, with half numb hand and whining dog. The result may appear less accurately as cleavers, but might feel closer to being there, looking at them.

This is what I want drawing to be, at least for myself: a record of being there as much as the making of an image. Drawing less as noun than as a verb in the present continuous.

25 January
Hard frost. No time alone to draw today, though I've packed a small notebook in my bag as usual, in hope of idle moments. And, as it happens, out walking I have several chances to draw as my children stop to investigate every type of frozen matter: hoarfrost, crystalline flakes, icicles, small frozen ponds. A new translucent ultramarine attaches to the four of us as our shadows slide across the ice.

We walk out of the town, into the fields towards the motorway. I watch my children rolling, laughing, on the icy ground, pretending to get up only to slip over again cartoonishly, then turn to look at the creeping thistle (*Cirsium arvense*) at the field's edge.

Thistles rarely invite sympathy; the name is almost onomatopoeic for their prickly rustle. They grip the ground fiercely and are impossible to seize by the stem and pull out. But the creeping thistle's seedheads have a dry and quirky stature I'm coming to appreciate like one might an eccentric elderly relative. It helps to know that its seeds are a significant food source for farmland birds, many of which are in decline. (They can be food for humans too – young shoots added to salads, and the hearts of the flowers prepared like artichokes.)

The overlapping bracts on the base of the flower heads remind me of tiled roofs; I wonder how many patterns and techniques of building were informed by plants.

Around the turn of the twentieth century, realising that much of what we might learn from plant structures occurs at a scale inaccessible to the naked eye, a German design professor built a camera that allowed him to focus a sufficiently clear macro lens on the forms of plants around him. Karl Blossfeldt (1865–1932) photographed details of stems, leaves, buds and seedheads in crystalline black and white, sometimes magnifying his specimens up to thirty times. His images reveal complexities of form and symmetry that seem exotic marvels, until you read the captions and find they belong to many of the most ordinary plants you might pass every morning: a stem of hedge-nettle, a twig of dogwood, an unfurling fern. Looked at today they still feel revelatory, even in a context where far more technically sophisticated image capture is taken for granted. There is a kind of extreme focus about them, an almost feverish concentration of looking. In many of the images you can see the focus just slipping away at the edges, and this makes the sharpness of the centre of the image even more distinct: visibly deliberate, finely tuned. The photographs convey an acute desire to see and to understand.

A sprig of Blossfeldt's comfrey splays out its flowerheads as ornamentally as an art nouveau gate; a row of horsetail shoots

Karl Blossfeldt, *Taraxacum officinale (Common dandelion)*, from *Art Forms in Nature* (Berlin: Ernst Wasmuth, 1928)

evokes pillars of finely fluted marble. Bleached of colour, the images emphasise form. Placed dead centre against a clear white ground, the symmetry of each plant feels 'designed', weirdly intentional, more manufactured than evolved. Other species reveal under magnification an almost uncanny anthropomorphism, like the trio of horse chestnut shoots bearing totemic mask-like faces, or the shoot of aconite emerging like a mop-headed boy, stretching himself awake.

In photographing these plants, Blossfeldt's intention was to provide inspiration and illustrate architectural principles for his students, and his images are a catalogue of riches in formal terms. But what gives them real weight, beyond the textbook, is the countering of this intricate symmetry of form with the plants' own unpredictable irregularity. However impressive a structure may be, and however beautifully it has been captured, if each of those facets of a bellflower, or ribs of an ox-eye daisy stem, or apertures in a poppy seedhead were perfectly even, we wouldn't care. It's the deviations from the rule than make them alive.

26 January

This time of year is a chance to see plants edited down to their essentials: the bare bones without voluminous foliage and lush petals to draw the eye. A lesson in anatomy, like Blossfeldt's photographs.* I want to store up these shapes as the skeletons of the drawings I will make of them in bloom.

---

* At art school in Edinburgh, an anatomy class was offered as an option for those of us interested in drawing from life (already considered archaic twenty years ago). The tutor wheeled in a creaky skeleton suspended on a frame and jabbed at its swinging bones with a stick of charcoal, pointing out where they would be seen protruding through the body's flesh.

At the edge of town I stop to draw at a hedge of brambles (*Rubus fruticosus*). We brought a two-year-old cousin here last autumn to pick his first blackberries. My daughter lifted him to the bushes, explaining which were ripe, which to avoid, reaching the higher fruit down for him, pulling thorny hoops away from his outstretched hands. These bare husks with the texture of worn, brown velvet may have held berries we picked. Next to them, a mass of dried-out drupelets are desiccated to hard black clusters, like a fly's compound eye: those that missed their picking, left to decay on the stem.

I shift my weight, nudging a stalk, and a drop of water falls from it onto my page, blurring the line, registering the moment. A few minutes into drawing, my hearing focuses or tunes in, in a similar way to my eye. I become aware of separate sources of sound, their approximate location and how they interrelate. Birdsong from the thicket; drops falling from the bushes; a mile away the warning bleeps of trucks reversing as drivers make their deliveries.

Back home I show my daughter the drawing and she relates the memory of her cousin straightaway. The bramble thicket holds the memory for us both, the chance to reach back to something experienced both half a year ago and countless other autumns before our time.

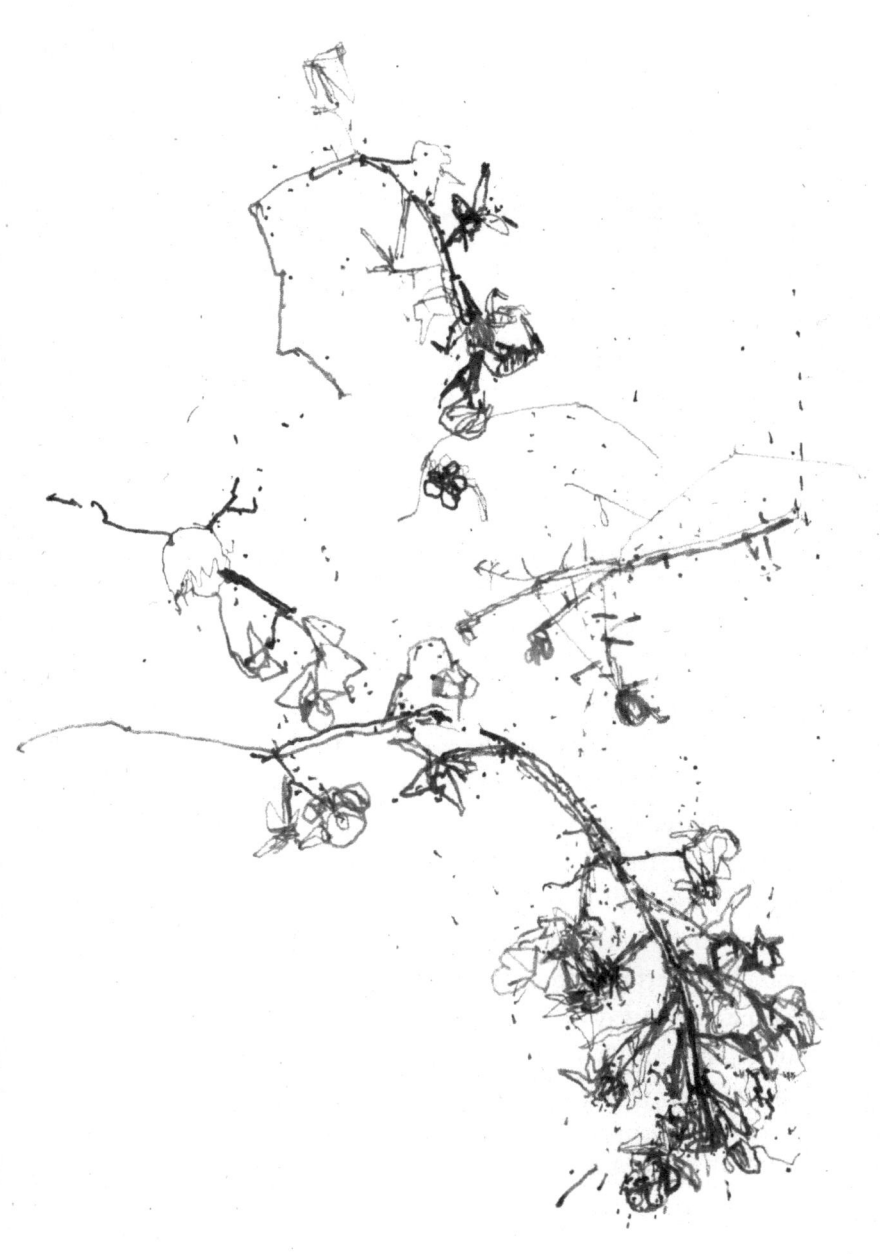

26 January: bramble (*Rubus fruticosus*)

FEBRUARY

> 'Do you think you'll ever make
> that drawing you do pay?'
> 'I don't think so, Patrick.'
> 'Why do you keep at it then?'
> 'It brings what I see closer.'

John McGahern, *That They May Face the Rising Sun*[6]

Here is a building I don't know, though I have been passing it for years. Windowless, surely more drainpiped than necessary, buff-coloured brick the texture of porridge, the door a choiceless dark green. In a 2-metre gap between the back of the building and the wall almost nothing can grow but ivy, and that's commuting in from somewhere else. Stalks of dead brambles crunch underfoot along with shards of bottle-brown glass. In the lee of the wall small rows of hart's tongue ferns crinkle up out of the dirt. Milk bottle tops, thorn-caught plastic bags, a baby's dummy. The handle of something, broken off. Odd clods of dark, dank moss the size of small birds, fallen from the roof.

Nothing and no one needs this worthless gap. The ivy gets in and runs amok. The sight of it – this wild, uninterrupted seizing of a chance – is a spur to something I don't know. I feel its energy course through me; I want to run.

2 February
The weeds are coming fast. Green is effervescing through the cracks, its volume amplifying each day, and those in charge have not noticed yet – or not enough to make a move.

Despite their lack of flowers, the tender pavement weeds now appear at their most ornamental – neat and flat enough to read as decoration. New dandelions, sowthistle and hairy bittercress radiate out from paving cracks in tidy stars, in patterns that yet never quite repeat. The minuscule appearance of a hundred pairs of leaves embellishes like lace. It's a Monday and I'm claiming the first hour of the week as my own. I'm heading out, bag packed with all I need: a pad of paper, clutch of pens, both fountain and dip, one of which should work. Bottle of ink bundled up in bubble wrap against a leak.

Here is as good as anywhere. Through earth apparently composed of rotting stalks, receipts and ketchup sachets, tangled stars of cleavers somehow make it through.

I choose to draw with ink because I want a mark that can't be hidden or erased, however uncertain it may be. Even a tentative line in ink is solid black; it registers each decision made, requires commitment to failing openly – and therefore cannot fail.

In practical terms, line drawing is the most simple and direct way of making an image, requiring minimal materials and no preparation beyond having them to hand. No need for a range of colours or graduating shades of grey, nor a

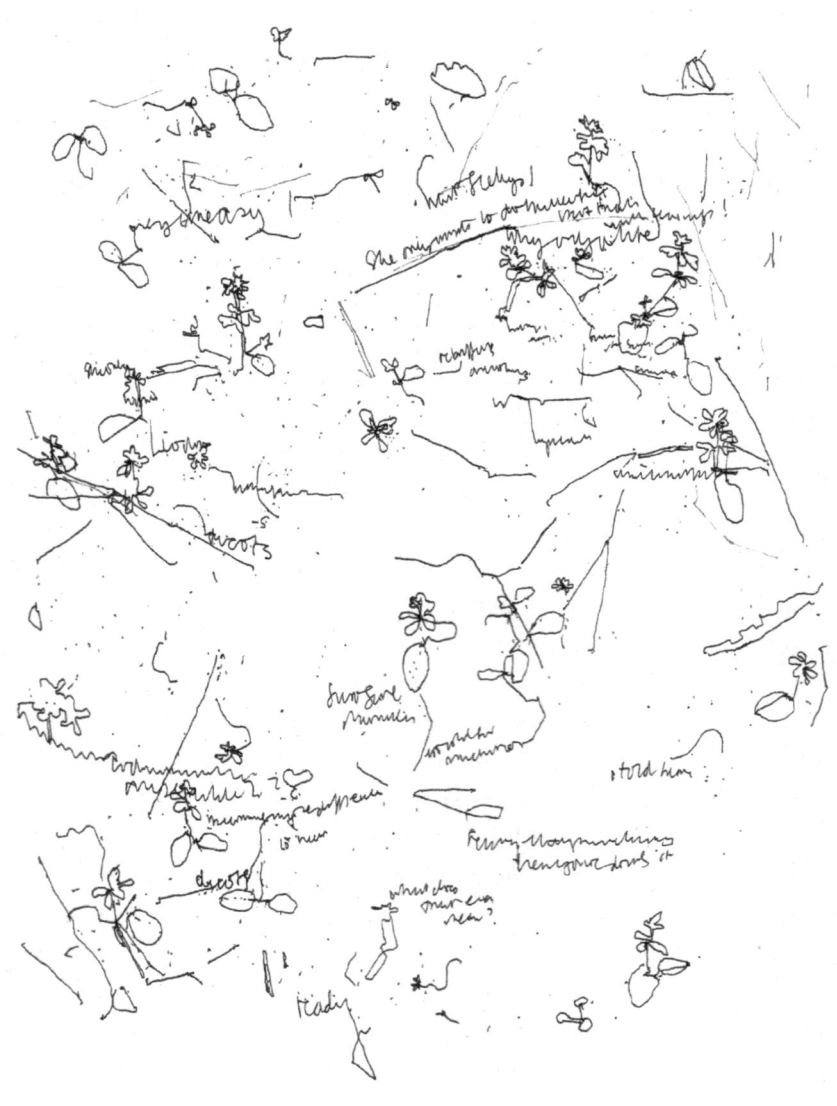

2 February: cleavers (*Galium aparine*)

specially primed surface, nor a plan of how the tonal range will calibrate to what's out there, nor how the layers of depth will be built up. A line drawing can begin in the moment of dropping pen to paper. Yet it's reasonable to argue that using tone, not line, would be a more truthful translation of what we see.

Few things I'm looking at are 'outlined'. Those fuzzy leaves setting out bright shapes against dull earth: it's the contrast which defines, rarely a linear mark. To describe an object with line – to delineate – is mostly a construct of interpretation, a mark of pragmatism or expediency rather than realism.

But it's the line that I want. Not convincing renderings of three dimensions, perspective, or even a sense of where the light is falling: what compels me is the setting out of outline information, without masking process in a persuasive account of volume. I want a drawing I make to look like a drawing: a response made line by line through a period of looking. I'm not interested in its purporting to be anything but drawing.

I need to stand and shake my feet, losing feeling in the compression of this up-close crouch. One-sided conversations of passersby bleed through the wall. Put a fist on the earth, avoiding glass, to steady myself back in place.

Something in the way these shoots respond to the mess they're in, circumventing rubbish and stalk-debris to push a way through, resonates with the struggle of what I'm doing. Confined to line, I need to find other ways to convey necessities of form and tone; a challenge which is different every time. All this adds complexity to the fundamental struggle of drawing. I'm dealing with a deficit I can't make up; the lines I make are ropes thrown out in hope of pulling something in.

7 February

Stop for a minute to draw a patch of wood-sorrel, emerging by the railings at the park edge. A low, creeping herb, wood-sorrel's leaves are *trefoil*, a word that sounds enduringly medieval. It's such a simple shape, three hearts joined at the tip, and yet from that botanical stamp not one comes out the same, either in size, generosity of curvature, or in the gradient of their central fold. Their outlines are so clear-cut they seem almost audible: crisp consonants that recall Gerard Manley Hopkins' description of them opening 'like some green lettering and cut sharp as dice'.* (Their taste matches this sharpness in its citrus tang.)

I find more lettering where ivy vines have fallen from a sycamore trunk, leaving slanting lengths of clinging hairs like lines of text. In the leaf-fall below, moth larvae make tracks of squiggly cursive across the veiny parchment of a leaf. On a nearby beech whose bark has absorbed past generations of carved graffiti, it's unclear which messages are human and which arboreal.

These meandering lines, made variously by cutting, biting, opening, tearing and falling away, produce a kind of text that can't be read; a wild, asemic manuscript of the place, made up of fragments. When it carries no meaning to be deciphered, such text becomes readable in a different way. The bleached cursive of the leaf-miner larva munching its exit through a sowthistle leaf depicts some distracted musing much closer to the mind's

---

* In a diary entry marked 15 April 1871, Hopkins allies plants with writing in other instances, too, describing grassy banks in May as 'versed with primroses', and the tops of elm trees 'touched and worded with leaf'. *The Journals and Papers of Gerard Manley Hopkins* (Oxford: Oxford University Press, 1959).

chaotic progression than a tidy line of text. Such rambling scripts can visualise cognitive uncertainties of our own.*

Like the leaf miner, I'm scrawling my own equivocal way ahead. As I walk through a wood, navigate the streets of a city or scroll through my social media feed, this last distracted path made via the upward flick of my thumb, I'm writing, daily, my own asemic text. More fundamental than any lines of words or weeds I might note down, my body's narrative is written in the broken twigs and crushed grasses of the understorey, the social and electronic transactions of the street, the Google tracking data my phone relays into the ether, and in the cookies cached in my online wake. There is nowhere I can go without leaving some trace.

'To live is to leave traces,' as Walter Benjamin observed; yet so much of life vanishes without. The trace of the leaf miner offers a glimpse of time captured in line.** Drawing is just a more explicit human attempt at doing the same.

11 February

Snowfall in the night. We wake to the heaviest frost yet: ice fractals on the inside of the windows that can't be believed until carved with a fingernail. Outside, the frost has inverted the colours, flipping dark stem to white line, pale stone to black ice. My phone's camera reads the snow as light and branches appear

---

* As Henri Michaux, whose asemic text-like drawings include *Alphabet* (1927), wrote in an essay in 1957: 'I wanted to draw the moments that, end to end, make up life, to make visible the interior sentence, the sentence without words.' (Quoted in Peter Schwenger, *Asemic: The Art of Writing* (Minnesota: University of Minnesota Press, 2019), 21–24; translation by Schwenger.)

** 'Our life is a faint tracing on the surface of mystery,' Annie Dillard observes, 'like the idle, curved tunnels of leaf miners on the face of a leaf.' Annie Dillard, *Pilgrim at Tinker Creek* (Norwich: Canterbury Press, 2011, 34).

backlit. Hairy outlines of hoarfrost on the ivy thicken each leaf more heavily on one side, making it seem as if everything has shifted to the right, a universal blur.

I spot new plants that I hadn't seen emerge: small beginnings previously concealed in the dun-coloured mass of dried-out stalks, their shapes now exaggerated by the frozen burr. The complexity of yarrow leaves is multiplied to insanity as each division is echoed in rime.

13 February
Snow is the severest editor. A field is now a clean sheet of paper. The blackened, metre-high stems of nettles, their flower-remnants brief taut scribbles, are all that's visible in the verge.

I walk with my family across a field of abandoned beet. Around the edges odd husks of last year's barley stab the air. Above us trembling quarrels of sparrows loop the field. Against snow-covered ground, buff tones of desiccated grasses and seedheads, which normally seem drained of colour, now reveal a palette of their own. Calibrated against white, the sedge becomes pale gold, the odd faint streak of green marking the centre of each leaf. Nettles are a darker pewter-fawn, dead cleavers dirty ivory shifting to pink. Woodier stems of shrubby weeds and brambles lend undertones of umber. Ryegrass is almost peach.

I crouch at the field's edge to draw a forgotten ear of barley (*Hordeum vulgare*). Wrapped in my thickest scarf, I can barely turn my head, my eyes are narrowing against the wind and I'm a blunt instrument for drawing. But the numbing cold lends a helpful urgency.

Afterwards, walking quickly to catch up with the others, I am alone and could be making use of the time to return some

13 February: barley (*Hordeum vulgare*)

calls. But I resist taking out my phone, feeling myself scanning the landscape with a keenness that I want to keep. I want to stay in the looking zone a bit longer.

15 February

In the small plantation half a mile out of town, I kneel against the bank to draw a new hart's tongue fern (*Asplenium scolopendrium*), one of the few plants to have come up in this part of the wood. For the first time in months there's real warmth in the sun on my back. It feels like a reignited conversation. Birdsong so bright and sweet it's sonically dazzling is punctuated by the staccato creak of a woodpecker.

Five small leaves, these tongues of deer held lapping at the ground, their surfaces a rumpled, rusting green, embossed by spores behind. I never knew a deer as a 'hart' until I met this fern. Many old words, replaced in common speech, linger on in the names of weeds.

I start to mark it out, but the place is marking it, too. The rasp of the motorway, more audible now without the trees' softening canopy, is curiously lulling. The woodpecker's intermittent bursts of sound prompt corresponding stutters of my nib. The slipperiness of leaf litter underfoot affects how I distribute my weight, my body's tension and control. However consciously I register such impressions or do not, a drawing made outdoors is always part-drawn by its environment.

18 February

I'm hungry for new plants. The plantation is only a small and recent bit of woodland; as the light stretches, triggering the dicots to pierce the ground, I want to know what's coming

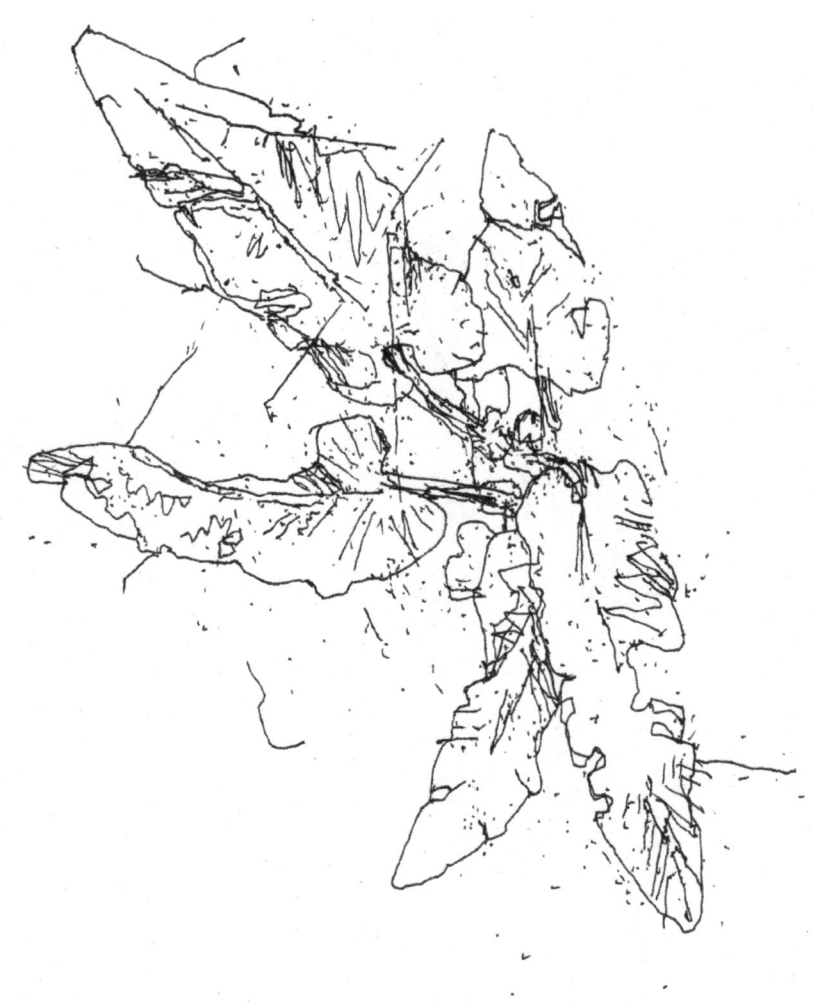

15 February: hart's tongue fern (*Asplenium scolopendrium*)

20 February: snowdrops (*Galanthus nivalis*)

up in the wilder places, further out of town in the wide, old woods where plants can spread undisturbed. I can't get out there yet – so I make do with reading about them. Dog's mercury, woodruff, wood speedwell, bluebell, wood anemone. Opposite-leaved golden saxifrage, a tiny plant that promises a citrus bite. All these are 'ancient woodland vascular plants': very slow to increase, their presence over wide areas can denote an ancient woodland (at least four centuries old). The spread of weeds marks time on a more-than-human scale.

20 February

The snowdrops (*Galanthus nivalis*) are the bluish-white of a new t-shirt with too much bleaching agent. Their petals – three outside and three smaller within – are held in a surprisingly firm green cap. Striations in green on their inside. On the outer tips that oddly digital green mark, a sort of bulbous V.

I sit with my back against a wall, drawing the snowdrops. My five-year-old son wants to draw the wall, but he wants to sit alongside me, too, with his back against it. Proximity is still a kind of gravity for him, whose force I sometimes underestimate. I start to explain that he won't be able to see the wall if it is behind him, then reconsider: why shouldn't leaning against something be a good way to draw it? Observation need not only be made by eye. So he begins. Then he sees I'm drawing the snowdrops around my ankles and wants to do that too, but almost immediately cries out 'I can't!' I look at his book. There is barely a mark. 'I can't do it!' he repeats. His eyes are swimming in information, he's overwhelmed and near tears. I remember once offering to rub his back and his inability to stand such stimulation, nerves feeling and relaying every sensation. Something similar is

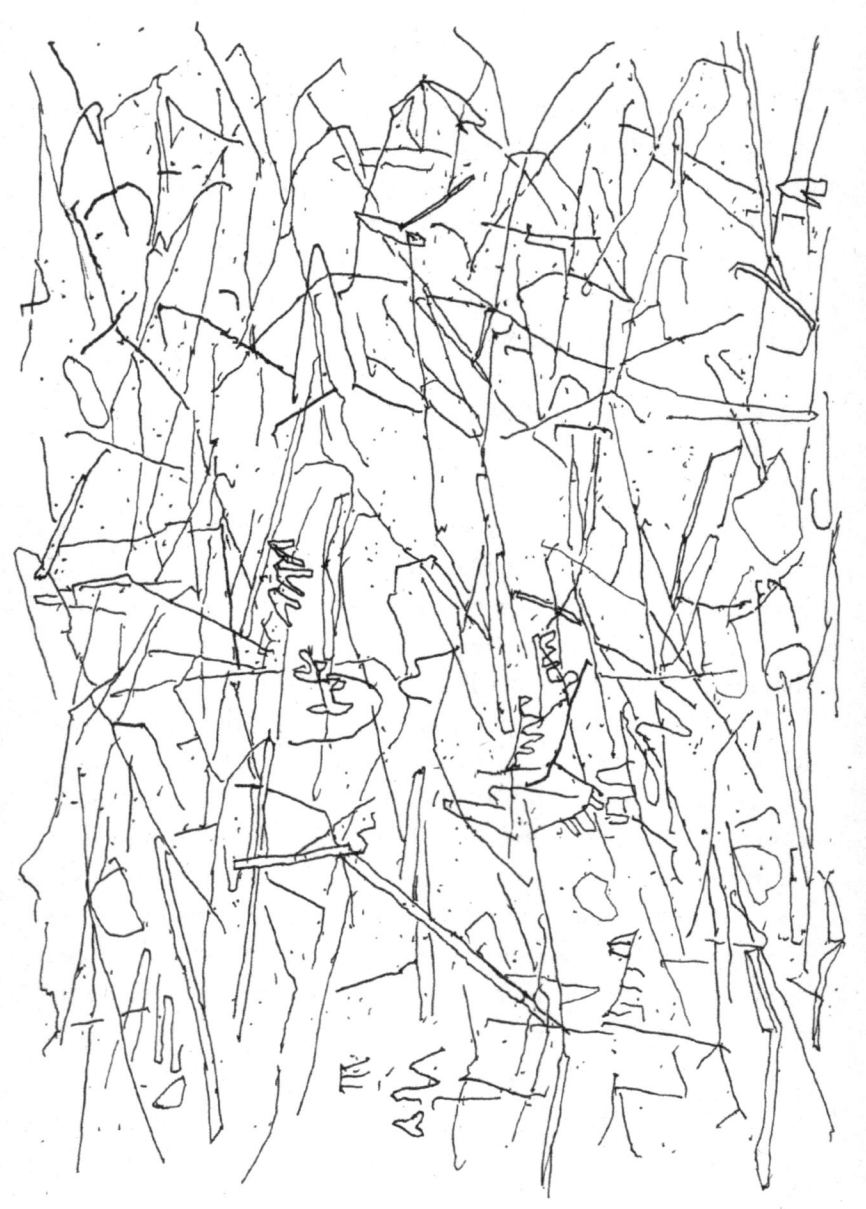

22 February: grassy bank

happening now. He is on his feet and, before I can say anything, stamping on the sketchbook. Damp earth spreads deep brown around the sides. 'Good! I want it muddy!'

I might have resisted the trampling but I've certainly experienced a similar frustration, countless times, especially when trying to draw too much. Attempt to draw a sweep of view even a few metres wide and you have to rely on conventions of summary. There is far too much information to equate each line or shape in what you see to an equivalent mark on paper: you must find ways of averaging, abbreviating, lumping together and missing out. This will involve recourse to established drawing shorthand – crosshatching to block in a tree canopy maybe; a tonal smudge for distant hills. And all this requires maintaining an overview of the situation, deliberately standing outside of what you are seeing. Literally and metaphorically, it demands perspective. This is why schoolchildren are so keen to learn the conventions – the lamb-shaped clouds, the sun in the top right corner with concentric rays, the trees with cauliflower silhouettes. They seize with relief on such simplifications, copying them from peers, because *actually* looking and trying to set down what you see can be overwhelming.

Why I have come to draw these plants alone, and not the broader sweep of landscape in which they stand, has to do with rejecting this summarising view. I don't want to construct my apartness any more than I can help. I want to feel immersed in the particular, in the detail, right among it: my heels digging into the soil, my elbow brushing the tall grass. I want to avoid as far as I can the instinct to summarise, edit, approximate – and, as closely as I'm able in the time I have to spare, to set it down line for line.

26 February: dandelions (*Taraxacum officinale*)

The main difference between my son's act of drawing and my own is our facility for filtering. I have decades on him, decades of learning to filter and to disregard, a gradual and necessary loss. If I had more integrity I should probably be stamping on my sketchbook.

21 February
First daisies in flower: white blots in the grass beside the carpark, more visible because they're still closed up. It's 8am; what time does the daisy call it day?

22 February
Waiting at the playground while my children play, I sit backwards on a park bench, feet through the gap in the slats, drawing whatever's coming through the grassy bank above. Various kinds of grasses whose names I will never learn, leaf litter, tiny fragments of fern. A perverse pleasure in confronting something relatively uniform, with little to single out; the concerted effort needed to keep track of where I am as my focus shifts back and forth from bank to paper, stretching the mind to its limits, but the effort having a rhythm to it, and just enough variety. A looping movement that fastens my attention to the grass.

26 February
There are, however, just as many other days when I can't seem to connect. When I stand in front of a weedy mass and feel too heavy to bring pen to paper and have to remind myself again that what I produce doesn't really matter. The point is not to produce a good drawing, only to be there and look. For a short interval, I'm putting aside everything else – all obligations and anxieties

of work, of parenthood, of domestic life – and worrying only at this triangular problem between plant, eye and paper.

This morning I head out weary and lacking conviction in what I'm doing. I stop and look at the budding bank. The visual information makes no impression, like an un-inked print. No optical kick to get me started. Well, OK; just begin. No need to work out a composition or to arrange the shapes on the page; start anywhere, wherever the eye and pen fall. Two new dandelions emerging, toothed spirals a couple of inches wide, a simple task. Faint pleasure starts to seep in as I work their medieval zigzag. *Dent de lion*, lion's tooth. A shape represented in artworks for centuries, perhaps millennia. My mind wanders to past incarnations of this shape, to a childhood book, to an idea for a salad.

Heading back, everything has shifted slightly, as if tuned into focus. Line and shape spring out of the thicket of weeds in the verge, lighting up strings of messages written in grass. I can feel my eyeballs darting.

The first dandelion to have been photographed, in the literal sense of written (*graph*) with light (*phos*), may have been a self-portrait by the plant itself: an image made without a camera on deep blue photo-sensitive paper laid out on the ground in the sun. The year was 1843. The technique of making cyanotypes had been invented a year before by John Herschel as a practical way of making copies (blueprints) of his documents and plans, but it was his friend Anna Atkins who saw its potential to make images that told a story of their own. A botanist, Atkins saw a means of recording plants more faithfully and objectively than any drawn image could, because the plant was registering itself.

Anna Atkins, *Dandelion (Taraxacum officinale)*, c.1854
cyanotype on paper, 35 x 24.3cm
V&A Museum, London

Within a year of Herschel's discovery, Atkins had published a book of cyanotype prints of native seaweeds which ran to several hundred pages. *Photographs of British Algae: Cyanotype Impressions* (1843–1853) is now regarded as the first photographically illustrated book, and Atkins as the first female photographer.

The daughter of a zoologist and chemist, Atkins had an unusually liberal upbringing for a woman of her time, with an emphasis on scientific learning. She made detailed drawings of shells to illustrate her father's books; she became active as a botanist, building collections of pressed flowers that she would later use in her prints, and by the age of forty she was elected a member of the Botanical Society of London. Her three-volume compendium of algae was followed a decade later by *Cyanotypes of British and Foreign Flowering Plants and Ferns* (1854), loose pages of which are now held in museums across the world, including a dandelion in London's V&A.

Like all cyanotypes, Atkins's dandelion is a register of touch; it records a series of careful actions made in the effort to see and understand and preserve. The dandelion has been picked near the base of its stems, its leaves and flowers placed on the surface of the paper and arranged quite judiciously, mostly avoiding overlaps, though one stem has been bent in a couple of places in the effort to do so. It has had to be flattened, small blurred areas revealing where this couldn't be perfectly achieved, with a handwritten label applied on a small strip of paper below. All this has been done with skill and care, but not, it seems to me, with meticulous precision. There is too much energy in the endeavour for that, too many other plants to catalogue. Earlier in her life, Atkins must have spent thousands of hours faithfully recording the details of her specimens through drawing; now, thanks to this strange new chemistry, she could do so in a matter of minutes. It's impossible to imagine today how that must have felt, and, for a botanist, how animating.

Like ink drawings, cyanotypes are essentially monochrome. The ink drawing uses black and the white of the paper, the cyanotype deep indigo-cyan and a less developed, paler turquoise where the plant lay. But the cyanotype reverses the usual image-making mark: the subject is registered as a negative, a deficiency of pigment. The process translates presence into loss.

An image's significance will inevitably shift with time. In my own photo-saturated period, in which I might snap a dozen dandelions on my phone without even thinking about it, Atkins's cyanotypes are no longer primarily botanical records. They are records of someone employing the limited language available to them – a language miraculous and beautiful in part because of its limitations. The cyanotype's blue makes its limitations explicit, reminds us that all languages, visual or otherwise, are movingly partial, only conveying what they can.

MARCH

> but I love flowers for their treachery
> their fragile bodies
> grace my imagination's avenues
>
> without their presence
> my mind would be an unmarked
> grave.
>
> Etel Adnan, 'The morning after / my death'[7]

2 March
I'm in Oxford for a day, and Google tells me I have twenty minutes, if I walk fast, before I need to be at the library for my appointment. I can see the Ashmolean Museum is on my route and decide to forego a coffee stop in favour of nipping in to see a favourite painting: Uccello's *The Hunt in the Forest* (circa 1470).

On my way up through the galleries towards the Uccello, though, another image catches my eye: a painting of a saint by an artist unknown to me, Altobello Melone's *Saint Helena*, circa 1520. In the bottom left corner, a small, nondescript weed

3 March: nettles (*Urtica dioica*)

has sprouted behind a rock at the saint's feet, and leans in the direction of her gaze. The more time I spend looking at weeds, the more I'm finding them lurking in the corners of paintings like this, even seeming to emerge from the crevices between the image and its frame. Perhaps the painters knew there was a fair chance their work would be cut down at some point, trimmed to fit a different wall or frame or altarpiece, as this panel was, and such anonymous plants could be a safe element to lose. It's as if the painted weeds, like their vegetal counterparts, are taking advantage of untended space.

When I get out my notebook and begin drawing the weed in Altobello's painting, a simple, flowerless stem of what might be purple toadflax, I see that almost every leaf coming off its stalk has been done with a single brushstroke. The thinness of the plant invites translucency; no need for repeated strokes of contouring. This brings a particular intimacy. To look at the plant is to look at a handful of small movements made by someone five centuries ago. I can feel them in my own body.

At this moment, the painting seems to me less a depiction of its subject than a repository of shared gestures.

3 March

The first new nettles are appearing – and now seems a good time to draw them, while they are only a few inches high. Already there's a crazy quantity of line and shape to make sense of; I feel my mind reach for words to pin it down, sort randomness into something recognisable. Struggling to explain the leaf shapes to myself I realise I lack the necessary language, and search Wikipedia for a botanical description.

The leaves have a strongly serrated margin, a cordate base, and an acuminate tip with a terminal leaf tooth longer than adjacent laterals.

Like the famously soothing shipping forecast, botanical descriptions can be a pleasure to hear even – perhaps especially – when their meaning isn't understood. Their economy and precision bring the reassuring sense that if nature is not under control, it is at least being catalogued and observed. And there are always detailed images to help. Accompanying the Wikipedia description is an emerald-green botanical illustration from the nineteenth century, a work of almost fluorescent clarity.[8] The illustration shines out of my phone's screen with absolute confidence: *we can work out what's going on here and report back*, it seems to say, leaving no leaf unturned, no room for doubt. There's just enough variation in the greens to give the requisite information – separate hues describe the indentations of the veins, ridging of stems, paleness of the leaves' undersides – but no other shades beyond those strictly necessary. The greens are dazzlingly bright, far more vivid than the grey-green plant I see at my feet, though whether saturated by the artist or by digitisation I can't be sure. My screen is backlit, after all.

I look down from the carefully serrated, illustrated leaves on screen and back at my own drawing. The former make an informative template, but the foliage of the plant I've drawn barely conforms. The zigzag edges proceed consistently but then change course; a straight dash follows, then a thinner tooth or rounded tip. The illustration charts a course, but drawing them as seen requires a much more errant line. And it's hard to see, in places where the leaves overlap, which saw-toothed edge belongs

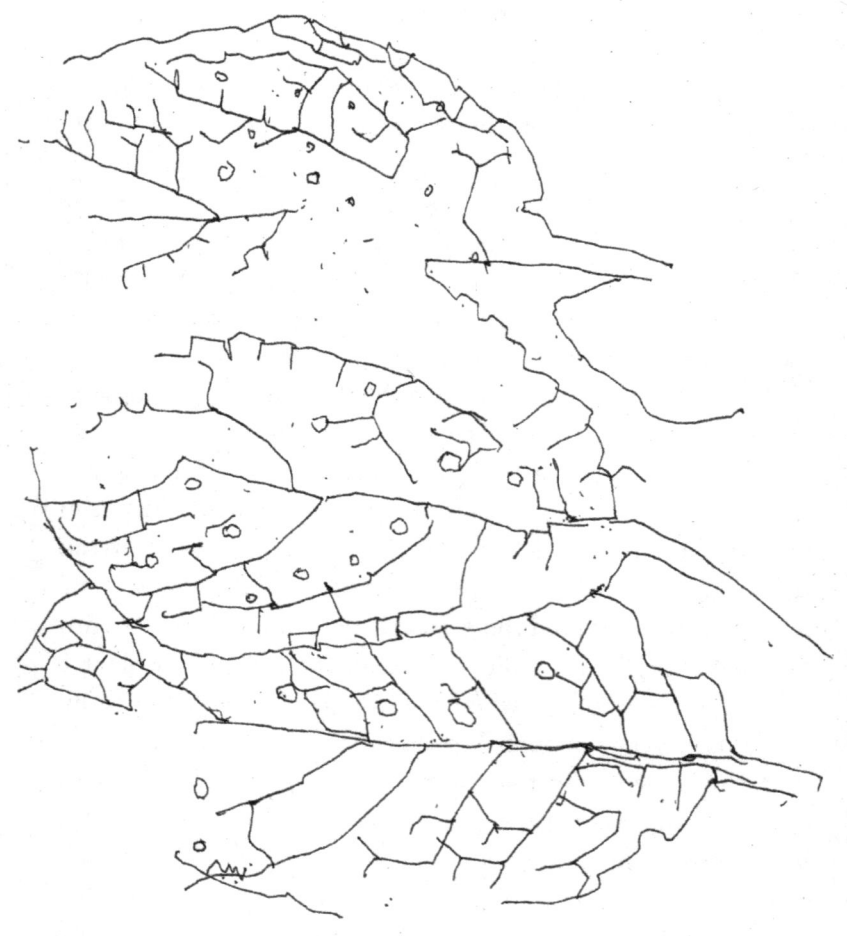

9 March: alkanet (*Pentaglottis sempervirens*)

to which. If I can't tell without leaning right in, and prodding at it with my nib, then should I make the separation visible in the drawing? For the botanical illustrator such explanations of structure are essential; for me, crouching in the grass, the best answer seems to admit my uncertainty.

5 March

The drawings are mounting up. The top drawer of my desk is stiff with sketchbooks, different sizes and kinds of paper for different weather, walk or ink. Some days I head out purposely to draw, or sneak in a half-hour around a work commitment, but I am finding that the best times are often when I'm supposed to be doing something else. Those lapses or kinks in the forward motion of the day, when intentions get derailed or stalled. I'm with my children perhaps, walking the dog or heading home from school, and they want to stop and play: I take that as a cue and look around to see what's coming through the ground.

Working in the interval allotted by their game gives me a sense of urgency and a particular, detached kind of focus, since I might be called on to stop at any time. In this, my children become collaborators who set the time and place; the kind of unpredictable determiners John Cage might have employed in his chance-driven compositions.

I hope that, from the perspective of my children, my nearby drawing is a good way of being unobtrusively present.

9 March

Since my last visit to this wood, a carpet of wild garlic (or ramsons; *Allium ursinum*) has pierced the ground. The glossy green spread reveals the forest's contours, smoothing over the details. Clumps of new dock punctuate, dusty with earth which somehow doesn't cling to the ramsons. I pick a handful of cleavers, young dandelions and garlic for a salad, stashing them between the pages of a magazine to keep them clean. My palm smells lusciously vernal.

The path curls past a weir. On its bank I find opposite-leaved golden saxifrage: a tiny plant my eye only picks out because of its sharp, acid-green flowers. Its round leaves are held, as the name suggests, in neat pairs, their scalloped edges like a child's drawing of a cloud.

Bordering the path, dark purple hoops of brambles overreach themselves. The scraps of leaves remaining gleam pale blue. The umbellifers' seedheads have fallen away. And, in the understorey, new leaves of alkanet (*Pentaglottis sempervirens*) are breaking through: bristly and deeply veined. I make a simple drawing of a stack of three, and a mental note to return in a month to find them in blue flower.

10 March

Today I fight the brambles and I lose. To state the obvious: most drawing paper is rectangular or square. This regular, straight-sided shape makes clear from the start that any marks made on it, however closely mimetic, represent a tidy selection of reality, a neat crop. The paper's edges act like the surveyor's quadrat flung on the ground. The portion of observed material recorded in the drawing may acknowledge the rectangle – extending to its edges – or hover somewhere within it, surrounded by white space, but in either case the rectangle obliges to greater or lesser extent some awareness of composition – which is to say, the intentional placement or arrangement of your image.

Bramble, of all the wild plants I have drawn so far, most shows up the restrictive artificiality of the rectangle. It's not just that my paper isn't nearly big enough to take in its scale. Trying to place the plant or any portion of it on the paper seems an absurd act of constraint. Everything about bramble is over-extended. There is no observable beginning or end to the plant. It arches up toward the light, it falls, it throws out suckers and re-roots, begins again. My drawing fails because it fails to excise my need to contain the image.

12 March

I'm behind on work – too much time heading out of town – but fortunately the weeds are emerging close at hand, too. In the shadow, literally, of my own doorstep, a seam of wild violets issues from a crack in the cement. When we moved here seven years ago I noticed violets in the nearby alleyway, and they have gradually made their way up to our door, spreading, I now know, via runners as well as seeding in the grooves between the paving slabs. I've been watching their dark heart leaves for months, and today the flowers have opened: a pale fluorescent mauve, darker at the throat, hanging down from their stems like lanterns from tiny hooks.

These are dog violets (*Viola reichenbachiana*) – 'dog' being a pejorative denoting inferiority to sweet violets (*Viola odorata*) because they are scentless – and they flower earlier than those scented cousins. Comparing the two species online, the dog violets seem tougher-looking, too, their stems stiffer, flower petals somehow scrappier, as if more carelessly drawn. To find *Viola odorata* I'll probably need to head right out of town; it grows in woods and shady hedgerows. But dog violets have a special charm for me, flowering in such intimate vicinity.

15 March: periwinkles (*Vinca minor*)

15 March

At the first bend in the river the land rises steeply upwards, held back by a wall whose outsize stones suggest pilfering from the nearby castle, perhaps when it was demolished to make way for the railway station. Shaded by woodland and carpeted with ivy, the bank is now studded with the bright mauve pinwheels of periwinkles (*Vinca minor*). I rest my notebook on the wall.

At this time of year, the ivy displays two shades of green: a verdant split personality. The darker and more solid foliage of previous years is tipped by a bright, soft green of new growth. Their difference is surprisingly marked and without gradation, and the new foliage can look almost plasticky before time and weather dull its sheen. There's a rookery above and I'm drawing to continuous cawing, a plaintive and peculiarly flat sound. The periwinkles, meanwhile, seem engineered to turn: each petal almost overlapping the next, and with a slight twist to its curve, like a tiny sail.

Each flower has a flaw – a notched leaf, an odd crease in a petal, a withered edge. Not one of them is perfect and yet each is somehow just right. I know this from drawing: if I try to make one up later, even a shape this simple will not look true. This is something I cannot explain.

A minute flurry of rain spatters the page. I close my notebook, but in the movement of leaving catch a flash of magenta behind the wall, half buried in the ivy. Peer further into the foliage: frayed petals, dark green plastic stem. An artificial lily. Just as I'm wondering how it could have got there, I remember the nearby bench where last year a grieving family made a shrine for their young daughter. My own children would stop to stroke the soft toys and read the cellophane-wrapped verses. Gradually the tributes and flowers had disappeared, some dispersed by the elements, others perhaps taken to a more permanent memorial. Nothing is left at the bench now, but blown a hundred yards behind a wall, this synthetic lily has taken root among the ivy.

A polyester hothouse bloom in spring woodland, the lily here is incongruous in almost every sense – in season, habitat, colour and material. Yet in other, imagined springs its unnatural appearance has long precedent. In stiffly beautiful medieval fields of flowers, the millefleurs of Flemish tapestries or Renaissance paintings, you might well find spring bulbs growing alongside late summer roses in the grass. These are not the happenstance places of our own world, they tell us. Anomaly and artificiality open up the space of allegory.

In Giovanni di Paolo's darkly luminous painting *Paradise*, painted in 1445 as part of a Siennese altarpiece and now in New York's Metropolitan Museum, groups of figures are reunited in a heavenly garden, and approach each other to embrace beneath an arboreal canopy. In between their reaching hands and stepping feet, each shady centimetre is crammed with jewel-like flowers: daisy, violet, carnation, periwinkle and lily.

16 March

I take the long route back from the shops and find a weed I haven't seen before, growing along a shaded path just metres from the high street. My plant identification app tells me it's a spotted deadnettle (*Lamium maculatum*) that looks like someone has brushed a white stripe down the centre of each leaf. The death in the name is because it has no sting, but its other sinister monikers – devil's clover, devil's nettle, double tongue – denote a plant marked out by some otherworldly hand.

Giovanni di Paolo, *Paradise*, 1445
tempera and gold on canvas, transferred from wood, 44.5 x 38.4cm
The Metropolitan Museum of Art, New York

16 March: spotted deadnettle (*Lamium maculatum*)

At the entrance to the park a battered clump of honesty still holds – the ragged discs like the shattered windows of an abandoned building.

I spend this first hour of the day following the tracery of veins in the deadnettle clump. But when I reach my desk, the next hour falls away to distraction. I am a slumped operator of devices and I shift my weight between them, now checking Instagram, now pulling myself up to my keyboard and tabbing across to a browser window, now responding to a WhatsApp or scrolling down the ragged-edged river of a message thread. I follow a line from a social media ad into a mycelial network of furniture outlets, many of them probably frontages for the same physical source; I follow several of these products, hypothetical purchases I am unlikely to buy, down the routes they would take, herding them into virtual baskets, checking shipping fees, promotional codes, rates of delivery. I close tabs and open new ones with a reflexive sideways tilt of my wrist, the shortcut-key gesture a muscle memory as deeply embedded as reaching for my child's hand. While this is happening I wonder, new tab, what has happened to a school acquaintance, whether I can book a certain train yet, tab, whether the changing weather, tab, will require a change of plan later. My phone alerts me intermittently to newnesses I can't locate, to things updating in its own unconscious background, working hard to keep my distraction fully operational.

The two phases of the morning might seem opposed, in quality of attention at least, but then again, I'm not so sure. Are drawing and digital meandering so dissimilar? Both involve a mix of intent observation and a certain time-oblivious fixity. In both drawing and online meandering, I move along a central course which branches off at successive tangents, the later side-shoots harder to trace back to the stem, but connected beneath the surface nonetheless. In each case I follow channels made by the movement of sap, one the water and nutrients carried through the plants' xylem and phloem, the other the juice of commerce flowing downstream to turn a profit. What might a drawing of the latter look like?

21 March
The river path is mottled with clumps of wild geranium: soft mounds of leaves that seem precision-cut. Further on I find a new patch of violets I have never seen here before. I reach to photograph it, but the image comes back as a weak excuse: petals bleached and diminished within the scruffy mat of ivy. Pale lilac is such a rare colour at this time of year it almost stings the eye to find it, but the camera knows nothing of this context and finds it pasty, unremarkable. As so often, the camera's objectivity reveals just how partially our own vision reports.

Everywhere I turn there's growth so vigorous and green I'm surprised it isn't making sound. Massive bunches of comfrey have appeared on the water's edge apparently overnight. The path is fringed with fresh spurts of mallows, already peppered with rust and insect quarryings. Mayweed embroiders the tarmac cracks.

New clumps of green encircle buff dead stalks, identifying the forgotten summer's stems as *Ballota nigra*, or black horehound. When will the old stalks fall away? Do they only disappear when subsumed by new growth, in the way that a memory will be overwritten by a fresh experience? More and

24 March: lesser celandine (*Ficaria verna*)

more I'm scrawling notes of plants to check back in on, in the weeks ahead.

Fumitory is back! My favourite riverside weed. The only one whose leaves still hold their droplets of dew.

23 March

A white dotted line along the pavement: chickweed starting to flower. Ditto hairy bittercress. Must return in a few days to draw.

24 March

Heading for the woods. A few of last year's brown leaves still cling to the brambles; they hang abjectly, like the corners of a mouth drooping, giving themselves up to gravity. But the hoops of the stems themselves are a gleeful game. A bend in the path reveals a sudden bolt of colour: old hawthorn branches dipped in mustard-yellow lichen, brilliant against the lacework of dead cleavers.

At the entrance to the wood, tree-shadows barcode the path. The floor is carpeted in lesser celandines (*Ficaria verna*), a dense and glossy covering of overlapping hearts; still no flowers. I wander without purpose, not looking for anything, stopping to sit on a bank in answer to fatigue rather than any intention, and decide to draw whatever's there.

This small, young curly dock (*Rumex crispus*) will do: a good chance to draw the plant before it gets too large and makes a joke of my paper's breadth. But already its complexity is intimidating. There's a huge amount of detail in each stem. I need to remind myself that I don't have to tell the full story of this plant – just one perspective at one moment.

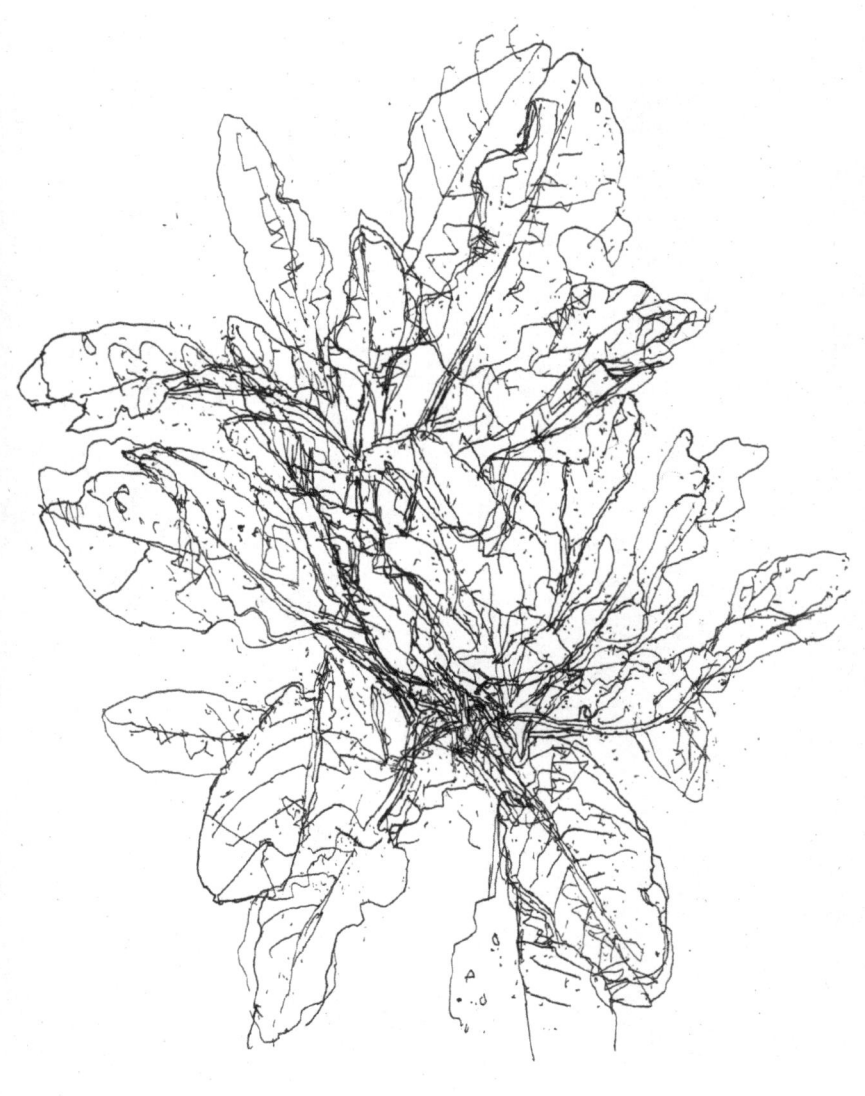

24 March: curly dock (*Rumex crispus*)

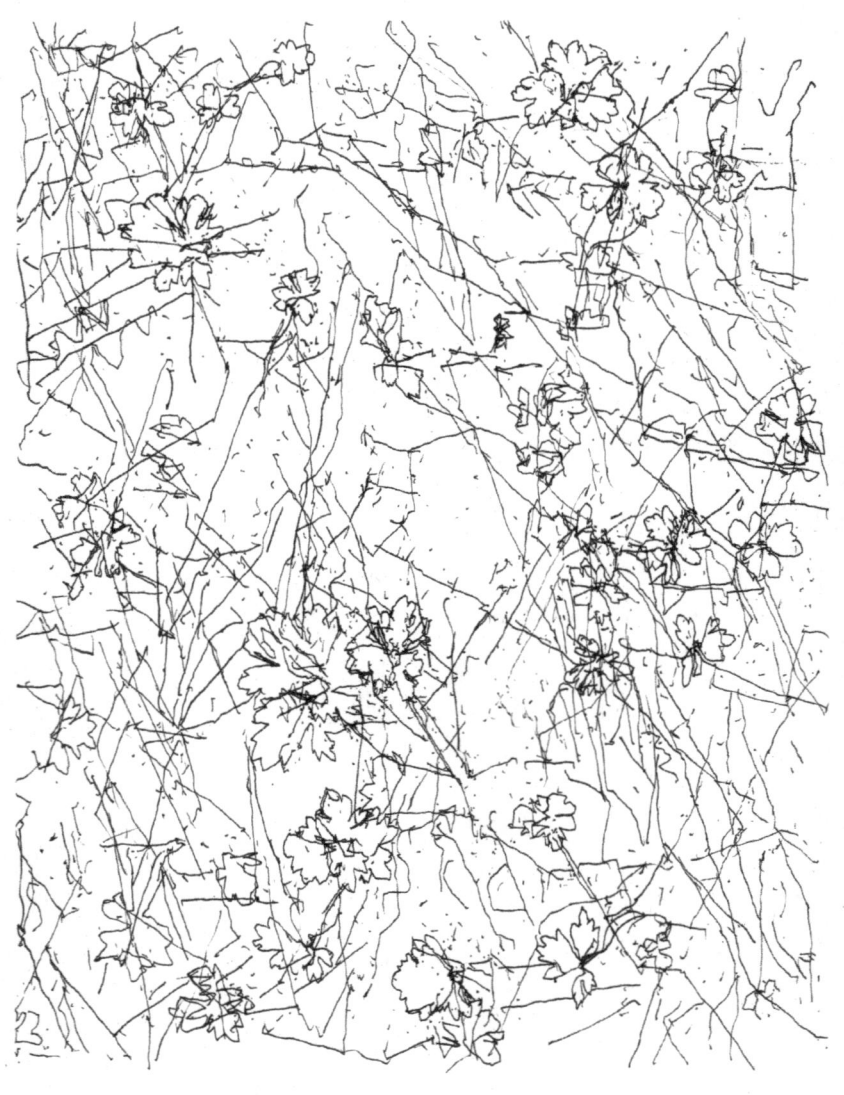

25 March: creeping buttercup (*Ranunculus repens*)

I learn two things from the drawing: 1) what looks like a single dock is really a muddled clump of several. I notice this only on looking at my drawing and seeing that the stems don't join up or converge at the same point. 2) imperfection is the rule, not the exception. Even the youngest leaves are puckered, rusted, nibbled, perforated, ragged. I wonder if there is any official outline to a dock leaf? I must look it up later in the wildflower guides, find out what the botanical illustrators conclude. But it would make no sense to depict one without damage.

25 March
Looking back at the drawings I've made so far, it seems that the best of them – by which I mean those that seem to me the truest – are those I've made against some urgency or restriction (weather, children, hunger). In these instances, I've stopped the drawing at the earliest possible moment. There is no fat or contented dither in them. On the other hand, when I'm dissatisfied with a drawing I've made, it's often because I've drawn too much, past the point of truly caring. I have stopped really looking at my subject, and instead of interrogating the plant, my attention has subsided onto the page. I've been thinking about this a lot and wondering if it means that *attention* is the same as *care*. Are the two mutually reliant, or can I attend to something when I draw without this care? My dictionary tells me that the two verbs can be synonymous, defining *to care* as 'to pay close attention'. And both words carry the idea of waiting, a need to stay with something, as the French *attendre* bears out. Yet this seems inadequate. I think of the poet Mary Oliver's observation, that 'attention without feeling [...] is only a report'.[9] To pay attention without caring has the flavour of duty. A dutiful

drawing, like a conscientious report, might be trustworthy – but would you want to look at it?

Mary Oliver credited photographer Molly Malone Cook, her partner of many years, with teaching her 'to see, with searching attention and compassion'. This seems a fuller definition of what's required – not just to stand by and concentrate, but to look with some kind of probing quality, and with empathy. 'An openness – an empathy – was necessary if the attention was to matter,' Oliver observed.[10] I realise that this searching quality can be felt in so many enduring images, of all kinds; it's there in Blossfeldt's photographs, in Atkins's cataloguing eye, in so many of the artworks that I love.

I'm thinking about all this as I walk back into town. Like a ruminating animal, the grinding movement of my thoughts turns over the familiar words in slow circles, breaking them down into something I can digest. In front of me the path slopes down towards a ditch, from where the field begins. The bank is smothered in creeping buttercup (*Ranunculus repens*).

I know that drawing's motive is not as simple as caring. If I care about every line I make, the result will be ponderous, heavy-handed. Some lines are better dashed off, set down with approximation, even impatience. Look at any verge. There's levity and springiness, ebullience – all deadened by a slow, too-faithful line.

I reach for my pen, wanting to make sense of it: the creeping buttercup on the bank overhung with errant blades of ryegrass, small ferns beginning, odd sprigs of cleavers and yellow celandines, beech leaves caught mid-fall, dank moss, all finding some imperfect tenure in the crumbling tilth. There are lines I need to follow with some diligence, and there are lines which must matter less. An upward thrust of a new plant seeking the light has a feeling of vertical intent. But the lines of dead grasses falling down the bank: that's gravity meeting the fact of the matter underneath; those lines lack the tension of intention, and it wouldn't be right, just now, to draw them with such.

It is the practice of responding which makes it clear: it's not about caring for every line. The care I take must be for the quality of attention, rather than the marks I draw. If I am attuned to what I'm seeing, there's little decision to make: the treatment of lines will look after itself.

26 March
Though I can't get as far as the woods I'm longing for, I'm heading out with my notebook more than usual at the moment. My mind feels particularly scattered. I crave the still focus of drawing, and the later comfort of looking back on the day's images, finding confirmation that I was there, did something, had agency.

On my way back from a meeting I detour into the park, kicking a way through the sycamore leaves on its margin. In among their papery brown, new hogweed shoots are coming through. I start with the lines of the sycamore leaves, their undersides curved like the ribbed hulls of boats. The hogweed is only a few inches tall but you can see how big the plants will get by the scale of their markings – every aspect super-sized, from the thick hairs on the stems to the fat, crenellated folds and fleshy profile. I don't find the right quality of line for them – they are not a plant with lines so much as folds – but keep going, grateful for the absorption until I've filled the page. Sometimes drawing is less an effort to care about what I'm seeing, and more about a pulling inward, a sense of drawing myself together.

29 March

The Polish grocery on the corner shut down a few months ago and the shop hasn't been re-let. Store fittings lie exposed in the window, various versions of off-white shelving discolouring and peeling in the sun. In the left-hand corner a strand of ivy-leaved toadflax has worked its way in through a crack in the wall to occupy the empty display.

Drawing in public, in the street in particular, can be a litmus for how you feel about yourself as much as the object you are drawing. It's exposing. You're stock still, narrow-focused, oblivious to your wider surroundings; easy prey, in a primitive sense. And if that's not noticeable enough, you're probably making some odd movements and squinting into space. Occasionally, this can get you into trouble.

One afternoon, aged sixteen, I walked out to draw in a field near my school, a place overlooked by few houses. It was so cold my colours were freezing on the page, leaving crystalline speckles in the paint's trail, and every few minutes I had to drop my sketchbook on the ploughed earth and run around to retain the sensation in my hands. Being engrossed in what I was doing, it was some time before I recognised the figure of a policeman striding across the mud towards me. Someone had called the station reporting 'a young person in some distress', he explained. I must have cut an odd figure, alternately stock still and circuiting the field.

It gets easier. Twenty-five years on, I avoid drawing on a well-used path or busy street simply so as not to get in the way, but I have few qualms about how I might appear to passersby. As we age most of us become less bothered by the impression we are making, but I suppose it's also the case that your concentration, when you draw, improves with time. You can pull your attention closer in to what you're looking at, and the self-consciousness will fall away, even if you have to do it again and again. You can lose yourself in the practice of looking.

APRIL

> How and why and where we classify plants as undesirable is part of the story of our ceaseless attempts to draw boundaries between nature and culture, wildness and domestication. And how intelligently and generously we draw those lines determines the character of most of the green surfaces of the planet.
>
> Richard Mabey, *Weeds* [11]

1 April

A woman is walking slowly and methodically along the edge of the street; she carries a plastic tank connected to a long black wand. She is spraying herbicide into the seam where the pavement meets her garden wall: the boundary of the row of houses here, edged verdantly with groundsel, grasses, sowthistle, shepherd's purse. By the end of the week her section of this boundary will be fringed with withering brown stalks. My daughter hasn't seen this apparatus before and asks her what she is doing. 'The weeds are damaging the wall,' she says, curiously.

2 April: daisies (*Bellis perennis*)

Weeds challenge our assumption that we can control our environment – and beyond that, as Richard Mabey has written, 'confront our sense of a purposeful, designed world, and our confidence in one in which we should be the major players, as of right'.[12] In urban areas, weeds are often to be found in the joins – between garden wall and pavement, or doorstep and street. We guard the joins and are alert to them; there may be a desire to take control of this vulnerable zone between private and public, to make clear or reinforce the division between the two.

On a domestic scale, the impulse to eradicate weeds often seems to be about their disruption of a quiet line. Irregular, unpredictable, the weeds mar and confuse clean boundaries, embodying disorder, an inability to 'manage' our lives, the triumph of chaos over order. Stone and brick and concrete are immoveable but this messy green line can be continually monitored and erased. For many of us, the action is instinctive, a gesture of control.

2 April

Saturday morning at the park. My children are now old enough to navigate the playpark by themselves, and I can sit in the grass at the edge, my back corrugated by the fence. Daisies (*Bellis perennis*) under my palms. Tiny suns, named *the day's eye*, since the flowers open with light and warmth and close at night.

Daisies' mats of leaves always look flattened, as if trodden on, but that's just how they are, how they get through winter. From above, the leaves are hard to put together into a plant, lying low and unambitious in the grass. Those flowers couldn't be cheerier but their stems end reticently, burying their conclusions in the sward.

APRIL

To draw a daisy is to draw the floral archetype: a bright disc haloed in petals, the motif of a child's drawing. Drawing something so familiar erases you: your hand is following a pattern so well-known there's little sense of agency. There are certain tricks artists use to circumvent such defaults, to prevent preconceived ideas about what things look like from kicking in. One is to ignore the object and draw its negative: the space around it. Focus on the shapes of air between the leaves, shapes which aren't familiar, about which you can assume nothing and must look afresh. You draw the gaps and gradually, unwittingly, the leaves appear.

Using absence to describe a shape is what Richard Long did in 1968, when in a field of daisies he picked the flowers that lay along two lines of an X, effectively making a drawing through removal. Long had made, and would continue to make, many other works in which his mark was made through walking. Here, in the silver gelatin photograph *England 1968*, Long's mark is not a path through but a halt, the cross equivocally an X-marks-the-spot, a target, a crossing out, a kiss. An X is both specificity and denial: it cancels itself out. Like Atkins's cyanotypes, the plant is here depicted by its absence. Unlike so much of the Land Art of the time, Long's gesture gently undermines itself, articulates nothing so much as the ephemerality of human presence. The artwork was recorded in a photograph, but the work itself would only endure until the daisies re-grew – which, being resilient weeds, they were bound to do. Long's work reminds me that the more effective mark might sometimes be an editing-out rather than an adding-in – and that some of the strongest images are made when treading softly.

*

Richard Long, *England 1968*, 1968
photograph, gelatin silver print on paper and graphite on board,
31.4 x 47.6cm [image]
© Richard Long. All Rights Reserved, DACS 2023.

APRIL

Another April, two years ago, in the first weeks of the pandemic: visiting my grandmother, confined to her room in a care home. The carpark is close to empty, gaps revealing for the first time a surprising expanse of lawn beyond. A4 rainbow clipart has been blu-tacked to the windows of the residents' lounge, its cheer belying the empty chairs, which lack their familiar silhouetted occupants. There's an atmosphere of waiting, and of quiet fear. The ramped entrance is now locked to visitors, and a pink-and-white plastic hand sanitising station fills most of the hallway. I walk around the side to the modern extension where my grandmother has a room, thankfully on the ground floor. She always keeps her window open – a lifetime habit even before she came to live in a permanently overheated room. The opening is now her only permitted contact with life outside.

I call to her through the window gap and wait a while, since she's almost certainly asleep. A few moments later she has pulled herself up and is slowly making her way with her walking frame to the window. I have about four minutes before the pain in her back makes it impossible for her to stand and talk. Once she has to sit down, she'll be too far from the opening to hear me.

'How are you, Gran?'

'Well, you know dear ...' she trails off, looking away. 'How are the family?' she asks, then leans more heavily against the sill, peering out at the lawn. 'Are those white things daisies?'

I tell her yes – they must be among the first of the year to flower.

'Ah ...' she sighs with pleasure. 'Do you remember making daisy chains? I used to make them with my sisters.'

For many of us, such interactions with weeds and wildflowers are some of our earliest physical experiences of nature, and among the most memorable, perhaps because they involve so many of our senses in combination. Picking a daisy, breaking that surprisingly tough stem, pressing a thumbnail in to make a slot that will be wide enough to take another but not so wide that it splits, taking a second stem and threading it through, pulling the flowerheads down ... It's several years since I've done it myself, but writing this I can feel the hairy stalk on the tip of my thumb, recall the careful gauging of where to place my nail, the split in the greyish stem breaking through to a wetter, brighter green. Sight, sound, scent, touch are intermingled – and even taste, if you like, since the flowers and leaves are edible.

That April my grandmother was a hundred years old. The white of the daisies, visible to her diminished sight as light spots on greyish ground, had carried her back across nearly a century of memory. I feel the daisies now under my palms, and let their fuzzy stems slide in between my fingers. This simplest of flowers, growing in almost any patch of grass from schoolyard to care home, is one that will accompany you from your earliest years until your last.

4 April

I visit C, an elderly friend, and we talk in her garden. My concentration lapses from the conversation in shallow dips as my eye falls on the weeds in the turf – coltsfoot leaves (*Tussilago farfara*), which in a reversal of the usual progression arrive *after* the plant's yellow flowers. These are the first I've seen. Wish it was socially acceptable to draw while talking. The talking would stop, of course.

6 April: honesty (*Lunaria annua*)

Under a hedge, small mounds of emerald foliage, so clear-cut they might have been carved on a pillar: the leaves of a yellow Welsh poppy. Next to it a hairy bittercress, flowering almost invisibly.

5 April

The weeds are like the scrolling text on TV news, proclaiming *this is live*. Or email spam whose constancy assures you're still online. I swipe across the news for some shot of newness or check on my messages for some sign of connection or meaning or proof that something matters. I swipe my eyes to the ground; the weeds assert: *just keep going*.

6 April

Waiting at the back of the chip shop for a takeaway, I find honesty (*Lunaria annua*) in flower, the first I've seen this spring. The flowering plant is so different to its seedhead that it's hard to imagine how the transition will occur: I need to watch for this later this summer.

Honesty leaves are nettle-like but broader, floppier and messier, becoming more so toward the base of the plant. Chalky-green stems darken as if dip-dyed, the ombré deepening to purple towards the top, a colour reaching for consensus with the pinkish-violet blooms. Each flower is a four-petalled cross; the outlines slightly wobbly, a shape drawn on a train. The petals seem to bleach in the sun, revealing darker veining.

Honesty is one of the few plants I can think of in which the seedheads – pearlescent, flattened ovals – are more recognisable and notable than its flowers, and both its Latin and common names bear this out. *Lunaria* refers to their moon shape, honesty to their translucency. Other monikers liken the discs to coins: moneywort, penny flower, silver dollar. I imagine them used as currency in generations of children's games.

9 April
At the corner of the street: last summer's nettles, dried to a weightless scribble, slowly being defeated by fresh mounds of zigzagging growth.

10 April
All over town new plants are making themselves known. New seams of spurges line the garden paths; buttercups lacquer the edges of our walk to school; the boundaries of the parks are a blur of cow parsley (*Anthriscus sylvestris*) readying itself to flower. It feels breathless. At last it's the weekend and I can get out to see what's happening in the wilder places, in the privacy of the wood.

The trees are greening up now and the canopy is thickening. In its understorey, layer on layer of plants break through the earth, circling in and out of each other indivisibly: elder, bramble, tree seedlings, ryegrass; beneath these again, dog's mercury, cleavers, golden saxifrage.

I pause to look at a patch of something on the edge of the path. It looks like a wild strawberry, but something's off, and my phone app tells me it's a completely different plant: a 'barren strawberry', *Potentilla sterilis*. Though the leaves are near-identical, this is a separate genus to *Fragaria fresca*, and, as I compare the plant in front of me with a true strawberry on screen, I see two tell-tale differences. The leaves of both are toothed, but the terminal tooth (tip) of the barren strawberry's leaves is blunted short. The barren strawberry's flowers, too, have a distinctive delicacy: five heart-shaped petals are held emphatically apart from one another, and the spaces between them read like a black outline, with the elegant pseudo-medieval grace of a William Morris pattern. These gaps prevent an easy rendering of the flowers, slowing my pen, making me consider each petal a separate entity.

Further on, a steep bank is a gift to draw. Too steep for footfall, nothing has been crushed, and all is lifted up to the gaze. A texture of incredible complexity: ground ivy, mosses, beetling insects, crinkle-leaved primroses, silverweed and sweet violets.

I lean in to sniff the violets' faint, sweet scent. Concentrate: you can only smell them once, or so the legend goes. This may be myth but it turns out to contain a scientific truth. The ketone ionine, a chemical responsible for the violet's scent, will temporarily deaden your scent receptors after you inhale.[13]

Maybe drawing can pin down what my sense of smell cannot. I make several attempts, but the delicacy of these flowers is on a scale beyond the finest I can work at. My pen feels like a bull in a china shop. It's like drawing the face of a very young child, when every line you put down ages them, seems an infinitesimal violation. (I have few drawings of my children as infants that I can face.) Their colour is similarly elusive. 'Violet,' Nan Shepherd wrote, 'can trouble the mind like music.'[14]

11 April

Down on the river path, the ramsons are in flower: white starry clusters top the wide green ribbon leaves, and a delicate garlic fragrance hangs in the air. The river is very low – no rain for weeks. Ground elder, mats of acid-yellow celandines, the flowers long-stemmed now and toppling; fine grasses pierce through here and there, and dock, looking old before its time. The first campion flowering. Alkanet's blue eye.

My regular walks are mostly routine – commutes to school and work, exercising the dog, the plethora of errands, odd trips to the station for a train. But as often as I walk these routes, the weeds will make them different every time. Like Heraclitus's river, the weeds mean you can never walk along the same street twice. Watching them gives purpose; the plants offer an intimacy of change, yet with perfect indifference to my response.

Today at the edge of a carpark I find a wide, dense stretch of ground ivy (*Glechoma hederacea*), several metres across. The violet flowers hit deep purple in the dappled shade. Just too small for me to see clearly, they seem to resemble miniature snapdragons, mauve petals streaked maroon inside. When two very similar hues appear adjacently like this, both look brighter than they would alone. The eye registers the difference as another impact; the 'not-quite' juxtaposition effecting an amplification.

At the top of each stem of ground ivy the burgeoning growth comes through reddish; its warmth transitions the eye from the green to the purple and seems to act as an echo or halo effect for the tiny flowers, making them more striking. I sit down to draw, inadvertently crushing a few stems and releasing their mint-like scent. Put one in my mouth to taste.*

Drawing these diminutive stems is showing me the limits of my eyesight. Without picking one and bringing it to my face, I can't see how the plant is structured – exactly how the flowers join the stem, how the leaves at the top are arranged, or how

---

* Ground ivy makes a good herbal tea.

11 April: ground ivy (*Glechoma hederacea*)

their surfaces are veined. I can't precisely explain it on my paper, at least not in any botanical way; I'm just trying to find as many shapes as I can to put down. In this way the limitations of sight can have the effect of abstraction.

It will have to do, for now. The understorey of my drawing is a taste; ground ivy flowering in my mouth. A dark, low-down taste, more serious than mint.

12 April

Dorothy Wordsworth, recording 12 April in her diary for 1798: 'The Spring advances rapidly, multitudes of primroses, dog-violets, periwinkles, stitchwort.' Exactly the sequence that I find along the river path today.

16 April

The wood is greening up. Every tree starts its leaves in a different way. The hawthorns are the first and freshest: so green it's like quenching a thirst, a visual drink of water after the desiccation of winter.

Green spelled the old way, *greene*, has an almost onomatopoeic quality – a spreading word that wants to be said with slow relish; a widening mouth, curling into a grin; a tree canopy expanding. Philip Larkin observes trees 'coming into leaf / Like something almost being said'.[15] That *almost* can't be there just for prosody; it's the not-quite-ness, the suspension or holding back from full communication which makes it so compelling. April feels like a widening of the eyes before May really opens its mouth to speak.

It's still early and the celandines are just starting to open for the day. With the petals half-closed, you can see their undersides are streaked, surprisingly, with raw sienna; they look like screwed-up faces. They are getting scrappier, in the way all the growth does, each mound interrupted by odd bits of twig and scrunched leaf.

I crouch down in the leaf litter to draw. At my feet, between two thick roots of beech, is a forget-me-not, the first clear speck of blue I've seen this morning.

18 April

It's barely 7am, and I'm walking to the station for a train. The path up from the river is lined with dandelions, but like the shops their flowers haven't opened yet. The curling bracts, usually pulled back beneath the flowers, now reveal themselves in place of blooms: an eight-leaved star the complicated mauve of an old bruise, closed tight around a chalk-green centre, with just the tips of yellow petals showing through.

I'm gradually discovering how variously a plant appears not only through its life cycle, like the honesty I drew last week, but according to the time of day. Dandelions are one of many common flowers to open and close at specific times – this diurnal opening having evolved in response to the activity of their pollinators and predators. Approaching the station, still stiff with sleep and mindful of the time, it's surreal to consider all these other body clocks at work alongside my own, each staggering in and out of phase, triggered by the light.

Plants follow circadian rhythms as our own bodies do. Their prompts seem to be a combination of factors, both external (mainly light) and endogenous (intrinsic to the plant). A study by the Japanese Society of Plant Physiologists, despite being conducted on the other side of the world, uses one of the commonest weeds

I can find in my own street: thale cress (*Arabidopsis Thaliana*). It reveals that the plant opens its flowers on sensing light, but its closure is purely determined by its internal clock. They are 'woken' by the sun, but their retreat is biologically prescribed. Perhaps without our clocks we'd be the same.

21 April

Emerging from a migraine, still screen- and light-averse, I chuck on dark glasses and head out. The right side of my head from temple to jaw feels bruised as if from a collision. Still in the disembodied zone, I'm heading along the coastal path to clear my head, and the track ahead of me seems to bubble up to meet my feet at unexpected levels. What is the grass here? Hiding in the plantain, pretending those corduroy leaves are its own, I find an unfamiliar white flower. I later identify it as scurvy-grass (*Cochlearia officinalis*).

I drop down to the street of houses where, three weeks ago, we saw a section of the wall being sprayed. Along its length are stands of luminous yellow mustard flower, sowthistles and dots of silk-red poppies. Until the section that was sprayed, where for some 10 metres the junction of the wall and pavement is matted beige. The remnants of the plants lie in soft collapse, strange, small peach-coloured heaps with darker, crisper fragments underneath. The colour is not the hue of dessicated stems that finish their life cycle in the normal way. It's something sweeter, like a colour pumped up by a filter on my phone.

The most commonly used herbicide, glyphosate, works by blocking the action of a key enzyme within the plant responsible for synthesising nutrients. The result is premature ageing, 'necrotic alterations' (changes to cell tissue) and rapid death. But the effect, of course, is not confined to the plant being sprayed.

And where does a plant end, anyway? In the drop of rainwater that runs off its leaves? In the bacteria that cluster around its roots? And what about the larva of the solitary bee which only lays eggs on nettle and thistle stalks, or the earthworm that shreds and disseminates the plant's decomposing form, fertilising the soil? We might target the plant, but the microbial composition of soil and surface water are affected too, as are the gut microbiota of animals – soil organisms, invertebrates including bees and earthworms, and even humans, through skin contact and inhalation.[16]

There is a widespread popular belief that weedkiller is 'safe to use', reflected in its casual recommendation by local authorities and its availability on supermarket shelves. Yet the World Health Organization's International Agency for Research on Cancer (IARC) has concluded that glyphosate is 'probably carcinogenic'.[17] Several countries including France have moved to ban its urban use. In Britain, the charity Pesticide Action UK works to promote sustainable alternatives, as well as campaigning for an urgently needed change in policy. A key challenge is the need to shift the widespread mindset that our urban areas ought to be weed-free.

24 April
I'm out walking with friends and can't stop to draw, but I note new things to come back for, breathing them into my phone in a slightly sheepish, witchy voice memo:

> yellow archangel – sheeny metallic markings on leaves
> hemlock
> greater woodrush
> wood anemone (white)

21 April: scurvy-grass (*Cochlearia officinalis*)

25 April: three-cornered leek (*Allium triquetrum*)

wild garlic and three-cornered leek both in full flower
comfrey clumping up
campion beginning to muster in clumps of twos and threes

We pick some Jack-by-the-hedge – *Alliaria petiolata*, a garlic mustard – to make pesto, but only metres away is a huge clump of hemlock (*Conium maculatum*), the poisonous plant that killed Socrates. Will need to check the leaves very carefully before adding them to the blender.

25 April

Wild garlic flowers are explosive. As so often in drawing there is a slippery negotiation between fidelity (getting the shape right) and spirit (capturing the feel of it). By the third drawing I've got my eye in and the balance between the two is nearer the mark. If I stayed here a week in the grass, drawing a single flower in a single stroke with my eyes closed, maybe eventually I'd hit it bang-on true.

26 April

A forget-me-not (*Myosotis* spp.) at the edge of the park. Experiment: I stand, pen-less, and try to follow the outline of a single cluster with my eye, stroking my focus around each curved petal, in around the bitten-out shape between the flowerheads. The eye's saccadic leaps are zanier and more uncontrollable than any other somatic behaviour I can think of, but I'm able to follow some of the shapes for a few seconds if I guide my vision with the slowing weight of my jaw. If I imagine drawing in this way just with my gaze, it does help me look for longer, but very quickly I start to sense I'm looking only to describe it to someone else. Words need to speak *to* someone, even if it's just yourself. Lines seem more autonomous.

I've been trying to find out more about this saccadic evasiveness of sight, and discover that we're neurologically incapable of looking for a sustained period – perhaps more than a few moments even – because the brain is wired to look for difference. If the eye is asked to linger on a fixed object, very soon our perception ceases to relay information and simply switches off. In the act of drawing however, the eye cannot stay still, but must keep darting to the paper and back to the object. This might be drawing's paradox: that it is only through looking away from what we gaze at that we can continue to see.

25 April: wild garlic (*Allium ursinum*)

MAY

The world is teeming; anything can happen.

John Cage, *Silence: Lectures and Writings*[18]

1 May

All over town new rashes of plants are taking over the flanks of the pavement edges, the crevices of the gutters and clefts in capstones, the overlooked behind spaces, the blind spots. I can't get out – or I'm out all the time but can't stop and take it in – and only rush past, squinting at the ground. Probably I'm no busier than usual, only outpaced by the drama of the surge.

Tonight, I get the kids to bed and nip out. It's after 8pm, but still light. Just a few yards up the street and they are all here: pellitory-of-the-wall, at its feet some tufts of ryegrass, sowthistles (beginning purplish), cleavers straining upward, ivy-leaved toadflax with its violet flowers at their brightest, sending out runners in wiry curlicues. Mallow, very small yet, shepherd's purse running to seed already, herb Robert, ground ivy. A little further and there's mayweed, thale cress. A few steps more: a perfect feverfew. All this within a hundred yards of my front door.

1 May: groundsel (*Senecio vulgaris*)

At the foot of a drainpipe is groundsel, one of the most ubiquitous plants here, which I've somehow not yet drawn. This is surely one of the lowliest weeds, its worn-out look reflected in its Latin name, *Senecio vulgaris*, which equates rather cruelly to 'a common or vulgar old man'. I prefer the vernacular 'old-man-in-the-spring'.

Groundsel has the demeanour of a classic weed, I find myself thinking, and I want to pick apart what that means. Take a step back. It's diminutive, growing up to 45cm high but often a lot less, and even the sturdiest young plants seem to cower or give in to wind and gravity. I put my pen aside and peer right in, trying to work out what's responsible for that shabby, aged aspect. The downy hairs along its stems, and the fluffy white seedheads – like small dandelion clocks – that give it the 'old man' moniker, obscure any smooth, neat lines. That tendency to lean limply or fall wonkily to one side, stems feebly bent under the modest weight of their flowers. Leaves lacking a consistently defined shape – their lobes either sharply or softly saw-toothed, apparently without predictable pattern. Small yellow flowers mostly hidden by their bracts, making them inconspicuous. Is it that a lack of distinctiveness or predictability tends to be read as disorder or disarray; that we are wired to seek pattern, and when it seems lacking, lose interest or respect?

Context plays a part too. Groundsel tends to root in the most modest cracks between wall and pavement, rather than in a field or open lawn, as if it's not worthy of any real territory but will just take what no one else wants. It's a manifestation of all those qualities we might secretly fear in ourselves: unremarkable, indefinite, unimposing, unworthy, weak. The kind of plant that makes *weed* a term of playground abuse. And yet it's one of the most widely distributed plants in the world, considered native in Europe, the United States, north Asia and parts of north Africa. Its spread is impossible to contain. Each small plant generates some 1,700 seeds; it is resistant to frost, can self-pollinate and will produce three generations in a single year. In terms of biological survival, the terms relevant to nature, it's an incredibly impressive plant. I wonder if its success and mediocre appearance are in some way linked – is it operating by stealth?

2 May
Groundsel along the wall collapse under the weight of their flowers. What seemed yesterday a weakness I now know is an evolved tactic – the curling over protects the flowers from getting wet, and once the blooms have gone to seed the stems will straighten to allow their downy fluff to catch the breeze.

Thale cress along all the seams of the street, flowering its socks off.

4 May
The first dandelion clocks have blown. Their stems present nubs newly exposed, sepals making a star-flower in place of the lost yellow tufts.

Along the river path, spring's pace accelerates in compound terms. Today's weedy litany, recorded into my phone: white deadnettle, ryegrass, nettle, sowthistle, crow garlic, mouse-ear chickweed, dandelion, daisy, yarrow, mallow, mayweed, forget-me-not, common thistle, wild geranium. All these within a 2-metre stretch, and I haven't even thought about the lichens, mosses and liverworts hidden underneath. The word *diversity* connotes so much that's serious and important, but the experience of it at a scale this intimate is just bewilderingly moving.

How can it happen, so many different species finding, in this silty crack of cement, their own space to thrive?

Around the corner from the undertakers, a confetti of cherry blossom has blown into the lee of the kerb, is softening and creasing into brown mulch, mixing with the other collected debris of the street that will gradually break down to form new soil. So little of this is needed to allow a seed to lodge and find the conditions that it needs to germinate. On the opposite street which leads down to the shops, the earth-lined gutter hosts a verdant fringe of grasses. Dandelions and hoary willowherb ornament the wheels of parked cars.

7 May

Driving to a meeting and realising I'm uncharacteristically early, I turn the car off the main road and pull up at a church in the middle of nowhere. The churchyard turns out to encompass the remnants of a medieval priory.

Five minutes after heading blindly down an A-road, I now find myself in a kind of open-air nave, car keys jangling in my pocket, schedule forgotten. The fragments of walls are little more than a metre high and encrusted all over with chalk-coloured lichens. A tall, blowsy weed is greening the cracks, rooting in the seams of age-old mortar, clinging to the contours of each crumbling profile. Its deep pink flowers halo every wall. This is red valerian – neither red nor, in fact, a valerian, but *Centranthus ruber*: a weed of ruins.

I've read that it's the alkalinity of the lime in mortar which the plant loves; the thoroughness of its spread over the stonework here is a kind of relishing. The little I know about pH is gleaned from gardening programmes on TV and bogus adverts for shampoo, and, further back, that uncanny colour-changing litmus paper of school science lessons. But this condition of environment that I'm blind to is a huge determiner for plants, the acidity or alkalinity governing what can grow and what can thrive.

Weeds in the cracks are embedded in our aesthetic of ruins. To take a paradigm: Piranesi's etchings of his *Views of Rome* (circa 1750–1778). Remove the foliage and those ancient ruined structures might appear half-built, not disintegrating. Weedy growth softens the built line, blurs carved shapes, draws attention to both the structure and its weak points, begins to return what humans built back to the earth. It's an oddly paradoxical relationship, signalling redundancy through fresh new growth.

The *Centranthus* here is a kind of deep magenta gone wrong, an ink shifting hue in too much sun. But the plant comes up in other colours too. Back in town it turns the quayside walls near where I live a lipstick pink, and I've seen a white variety at the back of the derelict community centre. Like so many urban weeds, its presence often signals a place that's out of sight, under the wire; somewhere you might be unobserved, too. For Derek Jarman, red valerian would always be 'a sexy plant' – the flower of the bomb-damaged garden his first lover took him to.[19]

8 May

In between the hummocks of municipal shrubs in the station carpark – the kinds of shrubs it's hard to notice, which seem only to serve the function of occupying space – a vetch is doodling the gaps. I love this tiny weightless plant for its stems' refusal to end. The stalks finish in a curlicue of tendrils which reach out and fasten onto their neighbours, so that the end of one plant is the beginning of another.

9 May: mouse-ear chickweed (*Cerastium vulgatum*)

9 May

You learn a new word and, in the days that follow, somehow hear it everywhere: this happens all the time as I'm learning about weeds – and of course the new plant really is everywhere, in all likelihood, since the move to identify it reflects its sudden proliferation.

Such is the case with mouse-ear chickweed (*Cerastium vulgatum*), a modest little weed with furry creased leaves and tiny white flowers that in the last week has appeared all over town in the cracks of pavements and lamp-posts, and here in the crevice of a wall, happily at eye level. The tight buds haven't opened yet and their shape issues almost by default from the slightly shaky, making-do gesture of my pen, though I struggle to get a line fine enough for the scale required.

A wind picks up and the flowers' tremble becomes too large a movement for me to discern their shape. I have to reach out every few moments and still the plant between my finger and thumb. All the time I'm drawing I'm aware of a constant shifting maze of ants beneath my sketchbook; a kind of madness.

10 May

Walk down to the river. Coltsfoot clocks on reptilian stems. Neon clumps of primroses.

In the long grass: a flicker of tiny white stars. I assume they are a kind of chickweed since the flowers are so similar to *Stellaria media*, the common chickweed; but when I look them up later, I find I've made a common mistake – an assumption corrected only a few years ago, in fact, after genetic analysis. The common name greater stitchwort still holds, but the Latin name is now *Rabelera holostea*. It is part of a completely different

10 May: greater stitchwort (*Rabelera holostea*)

family, the pinks, and the only species in the genus *Rabelera*.*
Even botanists, it seems, can be distracted by flowers.

The moment I put pen to paper, I hear a drop on the white sheet. I work quickly to get something down before the rain builds. Now I'm at the plant's level I see that its leaves are completely different to the common chickweed found all over town. The leaves are slim blades held almost vertically, like soft shards splitting from the stalk. Raindrops are beginning to catch in the joins. The stalks seem jointed at each leaf junction, making gentle zigzag leans which become more pronounced as the flowers mature. I see ten petals overlap, sticking together with damp; later research tells me there are only five, each petal splitting into two halfway to its base. Small missed details like this remind me that my eyes are beginning to fail.

12 May

On a morning where I find new blotches of sun damage on my face, I pass a clump of dock half mottled brown with rust. The mottling reads like a tarnishing of age, but the plant is young, a product of this spring. The rust is actually a fungus, *Puccinia phragmitis*, and though its name and appearance evoke the impairment wrought by time, it causes only cosmetic damage. I photograph a leaf close up, its surface filling the frame: bright spots of umber halo into deep maroon, expand into one another, veined all the while with the leaf's bright

---

* Stitchwort was used to treat stitch-like pains in the side. The sixteenth-century *Gerard's Herbal* records that 'They are wont to drink it in wine with the powder of acorns, against the pain in the side, stitches, and such like.' Quoted in W. T. Fernie, *Herbal Simples: Approved for Modern Uses of Cure* (Bristol: John Wright & Co., 1897).

tributaries. The pattern is something to marvel at, a design for the marbled endpapers of precious books. But step back to view the whole plant and it's ruinous again. It seems the outline demands the paradigm: we see a well-known shape, a leaf, and expect its ideal state of unmarred green. Zoom in, you lose the outlines and the judgement eases off, becomes a more neutral assessment.

'We tell ourselves stories in order to live,' in Joan Didion's words.[20] And this includes even the story of a dock leaf, and how it is supposed to be. The outlines we draw daily for ourselves, in order to tell our own heartfelt and necessary stories – just scribbled fictions, made to frame a wild and mottled inconsistency.

13 May

A bank of grassland around the corner from the school is criss-crossed with desire lines, like multiple and manic attempts at Richard Long's X. Nettles and white deadnettle, dandelions, stitchwort and buttercup thread through the billowing grass. Further on I find a first cow parsley in flower, held delicately on its purplish, jointed stems. Mad dance of plantains erupting everywhere, the tough black cones of their flowers knocking at our ankles as we cut through the grass. We're in the spring of Hopkins's poem now, 'when weeds, in wheels, shoot long and lovely and lush'.[21]

I take a different route home and discover a new plant: henbit deadnettle (*Lamium amplexicaule*). *Amplexicaule* means 'embracing the stalk' since its leaves clasp the stem directly, not via attaching stalks. Like chickweed, the common name refers to hens pecking keenly at its leaves. This is the third 'dead' (non-stinging) nettle that I've seen. All of them are edible, offering good hedgerow food.

I realise I can walk a path like this for years, and suddenly one May find a new arrival – a new grass in flower, staking its glaucous claim among the margin of cow parsley; sorrel speckling the lawn; a meadow vetchling hiding in the grass. And, equally mysteriously, something I assume permanently resident will quietly take its leave. 'The world is teeming,' as John Cage put it. Nothing is to be counted on happening, and yet anything might.

15 May

First time in the woods in a fortnight. Everything that's green is pushing through an almost invisible network of dead growth, mainly wood avens (herb bennet; *Geum urbanum*), whose lines end in wispy, velvety nubs, the remains of last year's seeds. The new growth is up to a foot high. Wiry, rust-brown stalks, their branching termini all that remains of autumn's docks, pull the eye down to the new growth at their base; even as the new leaves accumulate at the centre, their outer foliage has become as puckered as the skin on the back of my hand. Celandines persist wide open. The ferns' croziers are at their best, groups of them unfurling wherever I look. I crouch and find the quiet work of cow parsley pushing through the earth. Here and there a curling shoot, bent double, gives away just how they make it through – easier to break the ground with a smooth curve than the delicate tip of foliage. A child coming downstairs backwards.

The beech litter is beginning to subside now and reveals tired patches of moss. Hogweed shoots still reach along the

Selfheal, from the *Circa Instans* (Egerton 747), *c.*1300
manuscript on parchment, 294 pages, 36 x 24cm
British Library, London

horizontal, but the cleavers have begun their upward rush. A cluster of beer bottles is half-buried in the sticky stems, the extent of growth a clue to when the beer was drunk.

I have found pignut (*Conopodium majus*) here before and I'm back to look for it again. It's surprisingly easy to misplace things in a wood, or for previous findings to shift location in the memory, but I'm in luck today and find the patch almost straightaway. The dill-like fronds are beginning to raise themselves in relaxed curves, tips resting on the ground like pianists' hands poised to begin. I draw to birdsong sharp as light and, in the gaps, tiny rustling movements of things drying or expanding in the warmth.

Quite often when I begin to draw, especially in the early morning, a memory of the night's dream will seep into awareness. I wonder if some similar part of the brain is activated by both drawing and dreaming, perhaps drawing's flickering glance an echo of our dreaming's REM. Then again, perhaps it's just that I'm finally growing still. It happens now, and then the muted dream palette is replaced in my mind's eye by a manuscript page I looked at yesterday: a strange medieval herbal painted seven centuries ago in northern Italy, now housed in the British Library and known as the *Tractacus de herbis* or *Circa Instans*.[22]

This manuscript marks a moment in botanical illustration when the established approach of copying plants from classical precedents began to be questioned. For hundreds of years, illustrators had replicated images from copies of copies, resulting in flat, stylised depictions that had morphed a considerable distance from any original, observed source. By the late thirteenth century, new developments in painting were beginning to prompt manuscript illustrators to reach for a new sense of realism, and this meant drawing from life.* In the *Circa Instans* you can feel this bold and new attempt: a puzzling-out of how to depict the complex irregularity of a plant not only in some three-dimensional sense, but also within the container of a page of text. Stylised plants with their obliging symmetries fit a column's width more easily. But few images depicted in the *Circa Instans* match their allocated space; the plants spill out into the text as if still growing. Petals overlap paragraphs; roots extend down off the page as if in search of soil. A bindweed shrinks its leaves to reach into the gap between two columns, a wood-sorrel squeezes into the top margin, a verbena's leaf tips are abruptly curtailed. Some plants take over the page entirely, and the text has had to be superimposed.

Such disruptions signal an unsettled, unresolved approach that feels excitingly live. Whether due to the involvement of different artists or to the lack of availability of plant specimens, some of the illustrations hark back to the older style, and this makes the more naturalistic drawings seems brilliantly unruly. A dock, a dandelion and a hart's tongue fern are all presented with obediently spread-out leaves, arrayed like pressed flowers, neatly symmetrical. But a self-heal seems like something you might actually pick, with overlapping leaves and shifting greens, and the illustrator has abandoned any attempt to confine it to the allotted corner. Another page shows shepherd's purse top right, its leaves arranged in a stylish star-shaped pattern, but the

---

* Celia Fisher, *The Medieval Flower Book* (London: British Library, 2013). Fisher notes that the new realism began in medical schools in Salerno and was significantly influenced by Arabic art.

white bryony beneath has run riot and taken over the full page width, as rampant and fast-growing as any spring weed outside.

So many of the images seem not to have been pre-planned. It feels as if the artist began each drawing and was surprised by where it ended up, and how much space was needed. That sense of discovery in the making of an image, the privileging of curiosity over expectation, will always make a drawing feel more alive. The openness of it – the vulnerability, even – leaves room for a viewer's empathy. To find such spontaneity in an object as valuable and labour-intensive as a medieval manuscript remains intriguing and, in some timeless way, more accessibly humane. It's as if the images are documenting their own struggle to be made.

16 May

Stultifying headache, and despite my armoury of pills I can't seem to give it the slip. I put on my darkest glasses, pull a baseball cap as far down as I can while still glimpsing the ground in front of me, and head out.

The weeds are coming up so thick and fast that each day brings new arrivals along the river path that seem to have come here overnight, as if brought in on the tide. The campion is still going strong but starting to cede ground to a darker green of ox-eye daisy leaves, light zigzags of ranunculus and mallow.

There are pools of forget-me-nots pulsing in the shade of elders. Shepherd's purse is here, and new ragworts, and in the cracks in the stone more valerian beginning. Its confident pink will stripe the wall in weeks.

I stop at the bend in the river and drop down to draw whatever's there. A clump of ribwort plantain (*Plantago lanceolata*). The soft spears feel too definite for the energy I've got but I try anyway, telling myself just a few lines. The drawing is something to cling to, evidence that I have more agency than just this mute resistance to pain.

18 May

We are driving to a wood not marked on the map, and which, in any case, Google thinks is somewhere else. Opinions vary on its spelling. Though it's known quite well locally and we have been there many times, we often seem to take a wrong turn or, for some other reason, the journey takes longer than it ought to. It has the sense of a location in a Tarkovksy film, one which sometimes slips its coordinates. Maybe woods are always a bit like that.

This is a wood my grandmother would have called a thin place – where the air is 'thinner' and you might pass more easily between this world and whatever you imagine could be beyond it. We have come here now for the bluebells.

The English bluebell (*Hyacinthoides non-scripta*) can barely be described as blue. These veins that mark the centre of each petal are on the purple side of ultramarine; the flesh of the petals is a lighter, pinker mauve. Lilac? Violet? All the colour names I'm reaching for are already taken by other blooms. As the flowers age and fade, their veins retain their intensity while the petals pale, and you see the bluish streaks more clearly. Since each bud flowers and fades at a different moment, these shifts in hue are happening in micro-staggers even on a single stem; all this variation, combined with our disposition to read blue as distant, bring an otherworldly shimmer to the wood.

The scent steals in as I draw. If you sniff a bell you might not catch its scent; it arrives obliquely.

16 May: ribwort plantain (*Plantago lanceolata*)

No one would include the English bluebell in a list of weeds. For a start, it's far too discerning about its habitat; in the UK it is only really found in broadleaf woodland, and even there spreading with ancient slowness, each seed taking at least five years to develop into a bulb. Under threat from habitat destruction, *Hyacinthoides non-scripta* is a protected species, and trading in wild bluebell bulbs is now illegal. But its relative the Spanish bluebell (*Hyacinthoides hispanica*) grows with the haphazard adaptability and resilience of a weed all the way up my street, cropping up in local gardens and waste ground all over town. The Spanish bluebell looks and is a more robust plant; its stems stand upright and carry their bells on all sides, whereas the English flower bears its bells all on one face, causing that distinctive drooping curve as it curls over with their weight. There are other differences, too. *Hispanica* has broader leaves, its petals tend to be paler in colour and it bears no scent.* When I draw the latter in my back garden, I find its flowers open progressively down the stem in a temporal cascade. My drawing alerts me to this quality because the struggle to convey each flower's form is different from the last. The English bluebell's flowers are more unanimous.

Nearly five centuries ago, a man born not far from this wood, the parson-naturalist William Turner, described how English bluebells were used to make bookbinders' gum. He observed local boys 'scrape the roote of the herbe and glew their arrows and books with that slyme that they scrape off'.[23] The bluebell may embody the colour of distance and separation, but its sap, it seems, has the property of drawing things together, driving the

---

*That said, the distinction between the two species is not always clear-cut as they can often hybridise.

18 May: right: bluebell (*Hyacinthoides non-scripta*)
left: Spanish bluebell (*Hyacinthoides hispanica*)

arrow to its target, sealing reams of text into a book. I visualise the *Circa Instans* shelved among a hoard of other precious manuscripts in the British Library. How many of those ancient books might be bound together with bluebell sap?

20 May

Almost five months through the year, approaching a halfway point. The drawings I have made are mounting up, piles of them stashed inches high in the plan chest in the corner of my studio, shuffling into an inky thicket. This project of following the weeds has proved appropriately invasive, stealing across the territories of work, family and domestic life – so that now when we are out on walks and some wildflower catches my eye, my daughter warns 'Step away from the weeds!' But the drawing is as adaptable as I had hoped, too, fitting into narrow chinks of time I often couldn't otherwise use. It's giving me a reason to get out on days when energy or light are low, and a renewed interest in the repetitious routes of my daily life.

I am aware of needing to look for detail to latch on to as I move through the world, and this need, expressed through drawing, was probably a fundamental part of why I became an artist. Yet the detailed focus that helps me to observe the weeds, narrowing my gaze to them in the persistent way I must to draw, can have its challenging aspect, too.

Sometimes I notice all the wrong things. The streaks on the phone screen rather than the message. What's collecting in the corners of the stairs, not where or why I'm going. The problematic edges of a fried egg. A hypervigilance to what's moving in the corner of the eye: recognising it as trivial makes little difference except to remind you of your failure to keep perspective.

The details continue to flood in, presenting difficulties so small as to be inarticulate, and therefore unconfrontable.

In the grass at the back of our house the weather won't settle either; it vacillates, a thrum of sensation that can't be contained within that single word. Weather as whether, an expression of doubt. Nor is there any consistency underfoot. What's nominally lawn is composed as much of other plants: small pockmarked leaves of ragwort, daisies of course, undercurrents of clover and the odd desaturated thistle. As inside, the detail masses up, but here at least nothing is to be controlled or managed; nothing expects a response. I press my palms into the dirt.

22 May

A morning's walk on a high. Cow parsley at its zenith, strong enough for sparrows to land on, setting it quivering. The sense of overwhelm, so often a cause for complaint, comes as a rush of positive feeling. I'm taken over by inestimable green, the profusion of detail registering on my body. I stand on the edge of the path with my sketchbook, gazing stupidly, looking for lines, but the idea of line has been subsumed by mass, by shooting growth. My pen hangs uselessly in the face of it all. No drawing.

28 May

My daughter carries in her schoolbag a zipped case of one hundred coloured crayons. They were bought cheaply with her pocket money and as she deliberated in the shop, turning the transparent cylinder of them around in her hands, I could see that many of the colours were repeats. I mentioned this but she didn't want to hear it – and I shouldn't have pointed it out. For me, choosing drawing materials is about their specific qualities, but for her it's more often about the feeling of power or reach they give her as she carries them around. Now she will have all the colours she needs; she is prepared for any encounter.

I remember a similar craving for a wooden box spied in a shop window in my own childhood: a slim case of peach-coloured wood containing never-before-seen rows of colours, each small watercolour square cellophane-wrapped, like sweets. I held off from making any pictures for weeks until the birthday that would make it mine, because it seemed worthless to attempt anything with less than that full array of colours. I still have the ceramic palette that tessellated into the box.

My daughter doesn't suffer from my procrastinating tendencies. She gets going with her pencil before she has even rounded the corner of the kitchen table and perched lopsided on her chair, one leg dangling in constant motion, eyes darting around the room. She is compiling a book of butterflies. Each page of her notebook features a single insect copied from a borrowed field guide, bordered by its facts. Those crayons have the disappointingly faint, pallid colours cheap crayons do, but her pressure is so hard that the colours deboss the paper, each drawing's reverse side a mute portrait of her insistence. She draws everything like she really means it, and you need to hear about it too; she has no truck with uncertainty, and, I think for that reason, hates drawing things from her own observation. Her butterflies' symmetry is breezily approximate, but the pattern of each wing is crammed in fervently. Beneath each image is a paragraph of cursive, part culled from the field guide, part from her own longings. Her writing slopes urgently toward the spine, unbothered by the horizontal.

I sat down just now to write about the Spanish bluebells multiplying in the park. Thoughts of my children ambush me in a flood of detail, usurping my intentions, as periodically they should. When I write that detail down I can see it, plainly and embarrassingly, as love. But if the observation and its record are summoned by the feeling, the reverse is also true. It is the mass of observed detail, arriving in a rush or by slow incremental accumulation, that brings a sense of connection and care. Curiosity, environmental concern, the impulse to protect, can all be cultivated perhaps most simply by looking.

31 May

A difficult day, a family walk during which the friction between us is as entangling and impeding as the brambles alongside. Out of all ideas, I hang back from the others for a break, dropping down to the ground and reaching for my pen before I even look at what's in front of me. *Potentilla anserina*, silverweed, its saw-toothed leaves like foil ornament in the parched grass. I get out my notebook without purpose or enthusiasm, starting with the first edge of the nearest plant. The thought falls in: *enough to follow the outline of this leaf.* This is something I can manage. I'm not looking at the whole plant, nor thinking about composition or tonality or how any of it is going to fit on the page; just starting with the edge of this small leaf will be enough.

Part of the respite of drawing from observation can be this temporary release from decision-making. You cede authority to the object in front of you and relax into following its instruction. From the first mark, all you need do is put down as closely as you can what you are seeing. The plant will tell you what kind of mark you need to make, where it should lie in relation to your previous mark, where the next should go, and so on. You'll get it wrong, change tack maybe, but the scraps of incomplete drawn image will tell you to keep going. There's more than enough entanglement in that to occupy the mind. Other responsibilities, anxieties or decisions, all the trouble and complexity of being yourself, are temporarily put aside.

JUNE

> ... walking through a garden at night, when the plants come right up to the edges of their names and then beyond them
>
> Alice Oswald, introduction to her book
> *Weeds and Wild Flowers* [24]

> Every noun is a stump with its roots showing
>
> Derek Walcott, *The Prodigal* [25]

1 June

In the park today I find a stem of something I can't identify; back at my desk I realise I've deleted its photo and my drawing isn't much to go by. Without being able to name the plant, I'm much less certain that I will see it again. If it wasn't for the drawing I wouldn't be confident I'd seen it at all.

A memory from early childhood, forty summers ago: adults walking in front, trying to identify some wildflower or other in a garden, and the sudden realisation of what they were doing.

Attempting to assign a name. I remember this almost as a visual act – attaching a word-label to the plant, as if fastening a string of letters to it with a length of wire. How odd that seemed. Everything the flower was, it contained within itself, and yet the thing to do to make it known was to look elsewhere, to find something else to fix it to?

Now I'm muttering and clutching at those same word-tags myself; groping on a good day for the Latin binomial classification, more often rolling the common names, the enjoyably biting Anglo-Saxon epithets, around in the mouth. *Hoary mustard, bastard toadflax, stinking goosefoot, bristly ox-tongue*: they make good insults, many of them, like Shakespearean banter to hurl across a stage. Plenty of threats, too, carrying the whiff of superstition or the witch's curse – *devil's bit scabious, enchanter's nightshade, black medick*.* More gently prosaic, more innocently childlike, are the animal and bird allusions, where several body parts are often hyphenated together in the same plant – *mouse-ear chickweed, dove's-foot cranesbill* – like a surrealist game of exquisite corpse.** Or the allusions to domestic uses of a vanished age, *lady's bedstraw* to stuff a mattress, *teasel* to tease or raise the nap of woollen cloth. I learn that the suffix *-wort* (*woundwort, soapwort, nipplewort*) derives from the Old English *wyrt*, meaning 'plant', 'root' or 'herb', and was allocated to plants considered useful or beneficial. But there's a cast of oddball characters too whose significance can only be guessed at – who are all these *Jacks* and *Billys by-the-hedge*, and the poor old *hoary Alison*?

---

* Nina Edwards has noted that 'in its everyday name the function of or dread surrounding a particular plant is often laid bare'. Edwards, *Weeds*, 8.
** Also known as 'heads, bodies and legs'.

JUNE

I accumulate and retain these labels with mixed success. Some weeds seem to cleave to their name after I hear it only once, others slip out of naming again and again like a dog from its collar, or sneak under the moniker of another, in guise of superficial similarity. I use plant identification apps on my phone, their AI bolstered by a backup of kind and quirky communities, seemingly always on hand to view the snapshot queries of strangers. I trawl websites maintained by avid amateur botanists, or equally ardent weedkiller enthusiasts. I spend evenings scouring wildflower books picked up in charity shops, their cover photos sun-faded to cyan. I find field guides on racks in the street, apparently worthless now, or on the long-forgotten shelves of elderly relatives; their careful drawings present each plant on its best behaviour, formal as a school portrait (and, to my inexpert eye, often as hard to recognise). I go down the rabbit holes of blogs, scanning comment threads as unruly and overgrown as their subjects, zooming in hopefully on randomly high-resolution uploads. I want to tether this information to what I've seen. Identification is the gateway to more knowledge but it also increases your chances of recognising the plant again. The name's attachment to the shape retrieves the memory of seeing it more strongly. The nametag becomes a confirmation of experience, a sharpening of its outline.

And yet. While it aids the memory, identifying a plant by name, with all the associations it brings, more likely impedes the drawing eye. To observe and record what you see is always mediated by the influence of what you expect to be there, your seeing buffeted and filtered by previous experiences or preconceptions, and knowing a plant's name will only summon these with a louder call. This is why the poet Paul Valéry could say that 'to see something is to forget its name'.*

When Alice Oswald tells of plants that 'come right up to the edges of their names and then beyond them', I'm returned to the feeling of that first awareness of botanical naming four decades ago, and of its insufficiency. Maybe a name's relation to its subject is nearer to a fragile wire than the boxed-in heading of the field guide. Names can neither contain nor hold in place, only offer the fiction of possible order. Their suggestion of enclosure, of recognition or even management, can embolden a plant. A name can be a foil against which wildness overspills.

2 June

At the edge of the path, in the understorey of the hedge, a stretch of wood avens is threaded with brome grass (*Bromus* spp.). The plants are fully intertwined. There's no perceptible division between one plant and another; without running my fingers down each stem, I can't see where it begins, which leaves it owns, whether it's singular or part of a clump. The very concept of an individual plant seems a nonsense. Beneath them, smaller grasses linger in the depths; bare stalks of dandelions set seed, tangled among herb Robert, and new white deadnettles commence their ascent; lower still lurk mosses and small liverworts. The grasses bring a movement like speech, and the wood avens share their conversation; they too point and quake in every direction. Their leaves terminate by flushing pink as if they don't want to end.

---

* In fact, the source of this aphorism is uncertain, though it is generally attributed to Valéry.

3 June

Comfrey (*Symphytum officinale*) up to my neck. Its flowers hover across a spectrum from hot pink to its sun-bleached echo in palest mauve. Leaves and stems are fuzzy, almost stingingly so. Clumps of hemlock water-dropwort interject. Cleavers are secretly in flower.

More and more is coming up along the river path and I have no time to stop –

ox-eye daisy
hedge mustard
fairy foxglove
hemlock waterdropwort
herb bennet
hairy tare
crosswort
tansy

I've got none down on paper and they'll be gone before I get the chance, subsumed by cleavers and the ever-thickening comfrey.

The rush of growth continues. Along the pavements mildew sets in. The fungus powders the leaves, makes plants look down-at-heel, scruffy – or, looked at another way, adds new colours. Sowthistle's glaucous leaves gain a mauve lustre, its stems a matte and chalky glaze.

5 June

Excited to have found, for the first time, tares cropping up in the flowerbeds above the station carpark. My excitement is a twenty-first-century absurdity, since this is a weed of such age-old ubiquity there's even a parable in the Bible about it. But it turns out that the delicate, wiry hairy tare I've found is actually a vetch (*Vicia hirsuta*); the pestilent tares I've read about are most likely a completely different plant: darnel grass (*Lolium temulentum*).

Stories about darnel crop up through millennia of literature, with a common theme of abasement. In the odes of the Roman poet Horace (65 BCE), it's the poor food eaten by the country mouse whose urban guest eats lavishly; in Shakespeare's *King Lear* it is one of the 'idle weeds' the king has fashioned into a crown, denoting the loss of his mind. The parable in Matthew's gospel tells of darnel sown through a wheatfield by a vengeful enemy; darnel is poisonous, but, being indistinguishable from wheat until the ear appears, it cannot be weeded out. 'Let both grow together until the harvest,' the farmer wisely tells his workers, 'and in the time of harvest I will say to the reapers, Gather ye together first the tares, and bind them in bundles to burn them: but gather the wheat into my barn.'[26] Interpretations of the story are as various as you might expect from any biblical text, but the underlying metaphor is plain: on the Day of Judgement, when all is clearly seen, weeds stand for evil to be rooted out.

6 June
Instructions for drawing cow parsley –

Begin by calming your brain's objections, acknowledging the impossibility of the task and the insufficiency of your means. Find a couple of stems you can stand among without peering into sunlight, stinging an ankle or grazing thistles with your reaching elbows. Fumble for a pen among the grasses, lint and old receipts languishing in the seam of your bag.

6 June: cow parsley (*Anthriscus sylvestris*)

9 June: slender speedwell (*Veronica filiformis*)

Throw down some marks to connect this smooth white page with the tangle of stalks in front of you. Figure out how much you can include, between the confines of the paper, the sun's glare and the emails clamouring from the phone in your pocket. Resist the urge, for now, to plant your nose into those creamy umbels, to cup their domes in your palm.

The cow parsley is making drawings of its own, nodding increasing circles in the warm air. Its swaying loops shift the disclosure of its flowers, now lowering the discs to show them from above, now circling them back into profile. The movement makes drawing them technically harder but cognitively easier, keeping your eye alive in the effort to track the change.

Its ferny leaves require only a summary gesture, like grasping sense by following the intonation of a phrase. Individual words, leaves, are carried away by the flies.

9 June

So often the first memory of a plant lodges deep, persisting in the mind through subsequent encounters, and speedwell for me will always be the flower of bored PE lessons. Lying low, creeping about in the grass, the thread-like stems barely holding the flowers aloft, it keeps company with those who opt to be the distant dilatory fielder in a game when no one hits a ball that far.

This was probably the slender speedwell (*Veronica filiformis*), one of the most discreet lawn-lodging blues, but there are several others. Walking out today, I find the ivy-leaved *Veronica hederifolia* reaching foot-long strands down a shady wall, and in the verge at the corner of the street the more confident germander speedwell (*Veronica chamaedrys*), its flowers the largest and most noticeable of the three. It's this last which you're most likely to spy from standing height – no skiving in the grass required. All are native to the UK.

'Speedwell is a plant of the roadside which speeds you well; so in Ireland Speedwell was sewn on to clothes to keep the wearer from accident,' Geoffrey Grigson recorded in the 1950s, and *Veronica officinalis* has stems fine enough to thread a needle with, to sew itself into a jacket's weave, though it might more practically have been worn in a buttonhole.[27] Speed-you-well and forget-me-not: the hyphenated flowers of leave-taking, their flowers the blues of distance. Despite their clear differences – most obviously in the speedwell's four petals to the forget-me-not's five – in medieval Europe the plants were so closely associated as to be considered interchangeable.*

The speedwell's blue, like the forget-me-not's, is really a complex gamut of hues, even within a single flower. Each petal, already unsteady in its choice of blue-mauve-violet, vacillates further, on close inspection, between its background hue and the deeper purplish lines that streak the surface. A shade-lover, it lies in the shadow of grasses, whose movement brings infinitesimal flickering over the already unstable blues.

Those words I've used – unsteady, unstable, vacillating – bear negative connotations of weakness and indecision. But in colour such inconsistencies will amplify, rather than weaken, the perception of the message. An optical quirk of colour vision ensures that several versions of a hue placed close together will

---

* Celia Fisher notes that *ne m'oubliez mye* and *vergiz mein nicht* were used for both interchangeably. Fisher, *The Medieval Flower Book*.

appear brighter and more dazzling than a single, pure shade. The speedwell's flowers need to attract the flies to share their dust: in evolutionary terms, their colour vacillation may be decisive.

11 June

The lottery of pavement weeds: each species as common as the numbers one to ten, but their sequence and combination almost infinitely varied. A new relationship springs up between two plants ubiquitous elsewhere for months, and each becomes novel again. These maroon-veined mallow leaves I've seen since early spring read afresh against the cerulean forget-me-not. The weeds always bring pairings you didn't expect, and even in a mass of what seems to be one species there will be wild cards, anomalies; a syncopated rhythm of repeated stems surprises with the off beat of a random seed.

No time to stop and draw today, but time at least for a lengthening gaze; after a day staring at artificial light a foot from my face, it's a relief to let my eyes loose to follow the weeds greening off up the street.

15 June

By the back door I keep a cluster of herbs in pots. Each of them now has its weedy understorey, their shadows complicating the movement of the herbs over the paving. At the feet of the oregano: a tiny oxalis, inch-high nettles, sowthistle beginning and a delicate, sprawling chickweed. Underneath the dill: more chickweed and a diminutive red deadnettle. Here is the official version of events and the word on the street. The weeds, the guys who really belong here, will have their say and may drown out the party line. I'll pull some out to ensure the herbs can

15 June: sowthistle (*Sonchus* spp.)

persevere but won't be too thorough. In any case, I know they'll be back.

Today I take a break to draw a sowthistle (*Sonchus* spp.) next to the back door. I'm using a dip-pen, a chancey thing which makes the flow of ink harder to control. It gives an enjoyably scratchy line, apt for this spiky individual, and invites you to dip and press to get a thick and taut black mark, or wait until the ink has almost gone for finer, skating details. The need to work with the timing between dips of ink makes you move around the drawing more, too, finding the right area for the readiness of ink you've got; there's more risk, more chance of unexpected marks. It's another loop of complexity worked into the entanglement with the plant, another helpful impediment to automaticity.

19 June

We've almost reached the tipping point, the summer solstice. Now at the fullest part of the year, I'm often out of space and drawing just the tips of things, the flowers at the top.

Amid the new appearances each month are several constants. Cleavers, groundsel, nettle, at whatever stage in their quick turnover. Grasses, first dully dormant, now flowering in the breeze. Dandelions turning to clocks and beginning again. But perhaps the most ubiquitous of all, the plant that accompanies almost every walk, is the bramble.

I have made many drawings of brambles on my walks, but quickly found that the only way to draw them is to look at a detail. Those arching stems can't be contained on a single sheet of paper; they make the rectangle of a page absurd, and when I've tried a more distant view in an effort to fit the whole plant

Bramble, from the *Vienna Dioscorides*, c.512
manuscript on vellum, 491 pages, 37 x 31cm
Austrian National Library, Vienna

in, the drawing looks weirdly polite, which couldn't be less appropriate for this irrepressible, thorny weed. But there is a drawing of a bramble bush I've seen that captures it in full, and without any sense of constraint. It is an illustration in a herbal by the Greek botanist-physician Dioscorides, and it was drawn 1,500 years ago.

This manuscript is thought to be one of the first artworks we know of to have been commissioned by a woman. It was made early in the sixth century for Juliana Anicia, a Byzantine imperial princess living in Constantinople. Though created as an object of great luxury, the book went on to live through many more practical uses. By the fifteenth century it was being used in a hospital as a medical textbook, before passing into the hands of the Holy Roman Emperor in Vienna. It is now housed in the national library there, and is known as the *Vienna Dioscorides*.

The first time I saw the sixth-century bramble, its sinuous thorny stems looked weirdly familiar; I knew the angles of their curves exactly from my river-path walks.[28] The drawing seemed strangely contemporary and yet also seasonless. This bramble has leaves, but its main stems are wintry-bare; the tips are flowering as if it's high summer, but moving down the stem the flowers are replaced by autumn berries, like a time-lapse recording in a still image. The bramble stretches upward with youthful vigour, but its lowest shoot has already rooted and begun a daughter plant. Everything a bramble does throughout the year is distilled into a single drawing. And it still seems to be in motion, reaching up to the light.

This compression of multiple time-periods in the static image, which seems a kind of abstraction in art historical terms, as when the cubists found a way of showing the world from several perspectives in a single plane, is not such an abstraction if you head outside. Like many plants, the bramble sends out new green arcs above the silvering lapses of past winters' growth; some stems of in-between age still bear the desiccated drupelets of a recent autumn. Likewise, the honesty now flowering at the edges of the park raises purple blooms above the bleached straws of last year's seedheads. Nettles: fresh green growth amid old, wiry remnants. Different stages, different seasons of each plant often keep company in the same plane of place and time.

We don't know who drew the blackberry in the *Vienna Dioscorides*. It is one of 383 images in that manuscript, and their stylistic variety suggests that numerous artists were involved. The text is a sixth-century Byzantine Greek version of one of the earliest-known and certainly most longstanding works of natural history and pharmacology, *De Materia Medica* ('On Medical Material'). Written in the first century CE by Pedanius Dioscorides, a Greek physician in the Roman army, it was widely used for over 1,500 years until the emergence of new botanist-physicians in the Renaissance. There are at least two similar, later manuscripts of the same text with brambles oddly similar to the Vienna one: the same arrangement of flowering tips and rooting stems, an echo of the same familiar curves. It's thought that all three may have been copied from an even older book that has not survived.[29] The genealogy of these bramble drawings, their reoccurrence and growth away from an original, unlocatable source, seems to have a parallel with the spread of brambles themselves, and with the plant's own ability to regenerate and multiply from a fragment of root or stem.

On the right-hand margin, a tiny stem has broken off and hangs as if by a thread. It's there, in the same place, in each of the three Dioscorides manuscripts, and it's there on the river path as well, a tiny breakage echoing through the centuries.

21 June
Black plastic planters by the station like multi-storeyed bins, inadequately filled with pansies and municipal tulips gone rogue. Chickweed seizes its moment: within a week has filled the gaps, covering their embarrassment.

24 June
Forget-me-nots at the park. The forget-me-not is like the perfectly succinct phrase of its name, flowers gently clustered on its hyphenated stems, which seem to reach upwards in small exploratory jerks. I don't want to weigh it down with unnecessary adjectives or reiterations. Its leaves are shapes you will never remember. 'The buds start pink,' I find I've written on my drawing without realising it; a pink quickly forgotten. The flower's tentative posture seems to pose itself as a question: *Could it be this?*

I'm trying to hold back with my pen, to use as few ink lines as possible. John Clare got it down in only three: 'simple small forget-me-not / Eyed wi a pin's head yellow dot / I' the middle of its tender blue'.[30]

I've been reading *The Shepherd's Calendar*, Clare's year-long poem of rural life, for a contemporary account of the folkloric plant practices and uses I've heard alluded to – the children's games, holiday customs and love divination that linger today only as self-conscious quirks, if at all. *She loves me, she loves me not*, pulling out the petals of a daisy. A buttercup held against the chin, its lacquered reflection determining your fondness for butter. Clare's perspective is year-wide, but his viewpoint is right-up-close, near enough to sniff for scent. That spot in the centre of the forget-me-not's flower, 'a pin's head yellow dot' – that's not an observation made from standing height.

A diffidence, or comfortable neglect of punctuation helps too. 'do I write intelligable I am generally understood tho I do not use that awkward squad of pointings called commas colons semicolons &c', he conceded in a letter to a friend.[31] A lightness with the grammar that usually fixes things in place somehow works in league with his up-close eye to give that sense of a rush of observation, an immersion in detail, a view not from a desk but from down in the grass. Clare's full stop is in the eye of the forget-me-not.

So much of the looking that goes on in John Clare's poetry and journals seems suffused with nostalgia, both for a time before enclosure carved up the land he knew so closely, and for the idle freedom of childhood. His writing helps me understand the link John Berger makes between dullness, or having nothing to do, and a close knowing of things, when he writes that 'Intimacy implies having time on one's hands, even a kind of boredom.'[32] In my own time, when portable screens ensure that the experience of 'nothing happening' can be dismissed with one swipe, concerns are sometimes voiced about the need to allow our children to be bored, often in acknowledgment that boredom can foster creativity.* But isn't this another kind of prioritising of productivity? Isn't it also necessary, this unproductive waiting time, messing about at the park or in the street, just to feel that you've actually *been* there?

---

* Philosopher John Gray has observed that 'Nothing is more alien to the present age than idleness [...] How can there be play in a time when nothing has meaning unless it leads to something else?' John Gray, *Straw Dogs: Thoughts on Humans and Other Animals* (London: Granta Books, 2003).

24 June: forget-me-not (*Myosotis sylvatica*)

30 June

Down on the river path the verges are about to be cut. I walk a hundred yards ahead of the council cutters, trying to drink it all in. The dog roses are at their best, throwing out scent over several metres in waves that hang between the damper tang of elderflower. At eye-level here, drawn clean against the sky, the calligraphic upward strokes of grasses. But further on the meadow grass has reached its zenith and turns to sigh over the path.

The comfrey is burnt-tipped and drooping after months of vigour. Here and there a cow parsley stem unceremoniously folds in sudden, sodden collapse. The tall plants are ceding ground to new growth. Tansy is shooting up, its sharp-cut emerald foliage hiding incipient flowerheads frothing with cuckoo spit, and crow garlic explodes magenta orbs along the verge. Cross-weed has lost its tidy verticality and begun to run amok among the strengthening brambles. Hedge mustard holds magnificently upright, its wiry stems curling up like candelabras to bear the lemon flowers.

Mildew has set in among the groundsel and sowthistle, dusting their stems and leaves for yards ahead. These are the weeds that draw the council's blades. Their greens have turned scorched shades of browns and watery mauve that don't fit the summer's fresh official palette. Their thorny leaves twist wearily in anguished attitudes; the flowerheads break form, curl out of shape; their downy seeds bedraggle them, catching on stem or leaf as they fall, never blowing cleanly away.

Here and there forget-me-nots persist but their silhouette too has morphed; the stems present a symmetry of paired seeds. Their leaves shift shades of washed-out ochre and umber and green; their stems a pallid, indefinite maroon. The seeds, though purplish, are covered with pale hairs, giving them a powdery aspect. Very few flecks of blue flower remain. The lightness of it all, in movement and weight and colour, provokes the instinct to tear it up, accelerate the loss, clear all away. But only from the distance of standing height.

As the path narrows, a border of flattened ryegrass reveals red stems of cinquefoil, threaded with creamy petals. Splayed flowers of oat grass record the moment a firework turns and falls, shattering through nipplewort as tall as me.

30 June: annual meadow grass (*Poa* spp.)

JULY

In small things, delight is intense

Thomas A. Clark, *Distance and Proximity*[33]

1 July

I often photograph the plants I'm drawing – to check their identity later, to record where I found them, or to keep a dated record alongside my more haphazard scribbled notes. But it's also informative to look at the plant at arm's length, flattened out specimen-like on screen: the phone today's equivalent, perhaps, of the Victorians' flower press.

My photographs record how the plant comes out of the ground and in what company, what the terrain is like, the scale and colour, and a hundred other details I've edited out in my drawing of a single stem. In theory, this should help me build a fuller memory of what I've seen. Yet when I scroll through the rows of photos later in the day, they often seem to belong to someone else's walk. The arm's length ease, unlimited shooting and continuous feedback of phone photography can produce a curious provisionality. You're more there, but you're less there, too.

I still myself to draw a stalk of black horehound (*Ballota nigra*). The leaves start off the shape and colour of nettles, but mature to a dusty burgundy after flowering, a dull hue lightened by thousands of tiny hairs which catch the light. Their small-lipped whorls of lilac flowers glow in the shade, making me feel it's dusk already. As the petals drop, they reveal their casings as tiny, bright green stars.

3 July
I'm in the city for twenty-four hours, staying with friends. Between each planned activity, the weeds fill in the gaps. I'm curious to find what's growing here, amid the high-rent shops and heavy traffic.

We cross the park and everything looks close-cropped – the hedges, grass and trees all more noticeably 'maintained' than in my own small town. But weeds still find foothold around the edges. In tree pits and the longer grass between the roots of cherry trees, clover, chickweed, buttercup and shepherd's purse keep their heads down. In the paving setts around the pedestrian crossing, plantains, flattened by rush-hour commutes, collect a tide of bottle tops and chip-shop forks.

I walk down to the station through some of the city's busiest shopping streets. Very few plants survive this intensity of footfall, but green is stealing through the city's seams. In the shaded damp, small ferns collect in awkward slivers no one needs or wants; a buddleia seedling wedges in behind a drainpipe; chickweed makes a frilled collar around a railing.

At the station I find my train an hour delayed. I spend the time in the park over the road, filling a page with grass; the waiting disappears.

7 July: self-heal (*Prunella vulgaris*)

4 July

Home, and drinking tea on the back doorstep. In the cracks between the paving, wood-sorrel is in flower. The petals are so light that, even though no other leaf or blade of grass is stirring, the flowerheads tremble in a movement of air I can't feel. Their cool white is beautifully veined in violet – lines too fine for my nib – and translucent enough that the yellow pollen at their base shows through to the outside. They hang down, clandestine, on stems as fine as thread.

5 July

If I had to pick a favourite of the plants I've come to know this year, both in name and form, this would be it: the evocatively named fumitory or earthsmoke (*Fumaria officinalis*). This is a weed that emerges from the ground like a puff of smoke: fumy, as the name suggests. Its stems curl and creep like smoky wisps and the flowers are equally hard to grasp, their translucent pink tipped in black-maroon, as if they have been scorched. The grey-green softness is even lighter in the morning, when they seem to have an uncanny ability to hold the dew, and hence the light. The species name, *officinalis*, indicates that fumitory was used in medicine (Dioscorides recommended it to clear the sight) and it is still an important ingredient in the Ayurvedic tradition. But the plant seems to have been accorded more elusive powers too, inspired perhaps by its imaginative relationship with fire. The roots are said to smell of smoke: burn it in the house to expel evil spirits; and, if you are embarking on a journey, rub earthsmoke on your shoes to bring you luck.

7 July

Friends visit, and we head upriver to a favourite swimming spot. I make a quick drawing of a patch of self-heal (*Prunella vulgaris*) while the others are still downstream, their voices blurred by the river.

I'm thinking back to the self-heal pictured in the *Circa Instans*, a taller, greener plant than the abrupt stems in front of me, perhaps having grown in the Italian climate, or perhaps because the artist just didn't want to stop drawing. The simple physical pleasure of image-making on a day like this in high summer ... I'm sure this pleasure is hidden behind many of the 'choices' art history interprets as intention.

As its name suggests, self-heal has a long history of medicinal use for everything from healing wounds to soothing sore throats and treating heart disease. The reach of this plant – which can tolerate environments as various as this wet riverside in northern England and the harsh, parched plains of Texas – means its use in traditional herbal medicine is truly international. In Kashmir, a bath of self-heal soothes muscle aches; Chinese medicine uses it for liver problems; in America and Canada, the Algonquin people infuse its leaves to treat a fever. My pen follows the crenellated line of its flower bracts, their emerald green edged fuzzily in deep maroon. A few still contain their violet flowers: two-lipped, with a purple hood above and three-lobed petal below. I pick a handful of the flowers I've drawn to add, gently fried, to this evening's pizza.

8 July

At the corner of the street, new poppies in the lee of the kerb, hanging their heads in buds weighed down by their bunched silk. Improbably, the stems will straighten as they lighten into flower.

A few yards down, outside the new apartment block, a patch of ivy-leaved toadflax is gradually rewilding a square of astroturf.

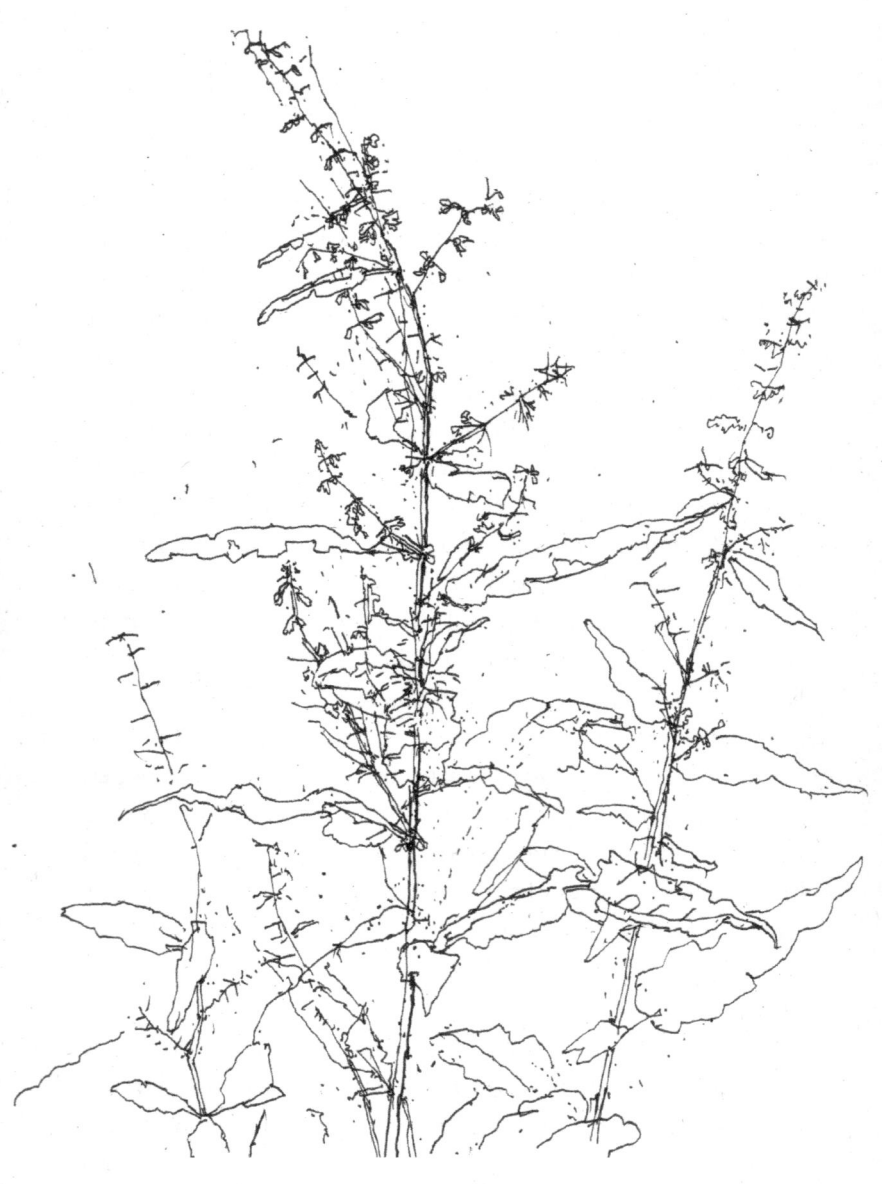

13 July: curly dock (*Rumex crispus*)

13 July

The nettles are all in flower: self-effacing, downward-looking threads of blooms we barely recognise as such. Nipplewort and woundwort complicate the grass. Cleavers gone to seed are threaded through everything, a weft to the warp of the upright plants, holding it all together. Sowthistle dots yellow here and there. Flowering docks, some green, some brown, are rusting at their tips. The odd campion persists, all the pinker for its scarcity. Bindweed's pale gramophones call mutely to the hedge.

I sit on a low wall by the bank of the river, legs hanging toward the water, my drawing paper protesting against my elbow in the gathering breeze. The grasses here are woven with soft, cream meadowsweet and white nettle-leaved bellflower (*Campanula trachelium*), whose elongated bells hit an almost ultra-violet white, the hi-white of photocopy paper.* It's an odd combination of highlights, like a fluorescent bulb next to an open window.

Trying to draw plants in the wind is an invitation to accept failure, to anticipate getting it wrong and adjusting your view as part of the process. The plant will not hold still; the angle of each stem will continue to shift, both in relation to the vertical and to its neighbour. Persisting with the drawing involves, paradoxically, a kind of relaxing into this. It's a slippery balance between caring in the moment and yet not minding how the drawing turns out. To be true to the plant in front of me, I have to fail to record it clearly.

Yet, in another sense, the breeze just stirs up the failure inherent in the act of drawing. 'Drawing is a constant correcting

---

* The flowers are more commonly violet; this white is unusual.

of errors. Maybe a great deal of creation is actually that,' John Berger observed, discussing his own exploration of the practice in *Bento's Sketchbook*.[34] Many of those errors occur before the ink touches the paper, and are corrected in the mind before a mark is set down. Any finished drawing exhibits an echo of all the greater, louder errors and failures that died out during its making.

14 July

Behind the railings, opposite the coffee shop: a complete enmeshing of dog rose and bramble. The flowers of both are creamy white just tinged with pink, roundly open with a thick cluster of stamens for the bees who work their way around as I look. Are they attracting the same pollinators? Both belong to the rose family. It feels like a collaboration between the two plants, though I know that's anthropomorphising.

16 July

The most interesting thing going on in the back garden is in an ugly ceramic pot I found today at the back of the hedge. The pot was left here by a previous owner and I'd intended to smash it up, recycling it into crocks for other planters, but at some point last summer I must have needed a place to put a supermarket sage, hurriedly planted it there and forgot about it. Left untended the sage has grown tall and woody, and its sparse leaves cling to twiggy stems exposed in awkward attitudes, like a drawing done with the left hand. Yet this awkwardness somehow lends a peculiar grace. Threaded through the parched-grey stems a handful of fresh weeds are coming up: ferny arcs of yarrow, a diminutive groundsel and, new to me, a glowing, chalk-white sneezewort (*Achillea ptarmica*) whose double flowers tilt toward the light.

13 July: nettle-leaved bellflower (*Campanula trachelium*)

A garden pot like this is usually intended as a focus, placed in some prime spot by a front door. So a pot taken over by weeds tells a very human tale of intention and lassitude, optimism and passivity, effort and overwhelm. It's a tale told down almost any street, and there are usually several pots like this in my garden, in addition to a few that I manage to maintain – watering enough, deadheading, cutting back. But finding the sage-yarrow-sneezewort here reminds me that, so often with plants, it is the failure of what was intended that can provide the most delight. It is a truism in art-making that 'practice saves you from the poverty of your intentions'. The same might well be said of weeds.

17 July
Meadow buttercups (*Ranunculis acris*) – the petals drop and leave behind the craziest seedheads: globular and covered in reddish spines like a wig.

18 July
Behind the station, the railtracks are edged in streams of perennial sowthistle (*Sonchus arvensis*). Its flowers are like the common dandelion but it's much taller, over a metre high. The leaves too have a dandelion's toothed outline but are spiky all over. I stand with pen hovering, reluctant to confront a quantity of foliage so dense and disproportionate to the time I have and my usual expectations of what's reasonable to include.

Just begin and see what happens. I start to track an inflorescence shimmering with black thunderbugs. The flowers present flattened suns back to the sky. Their colour warms to yolk-orange toward the centre; those still in bud present their crinkled petals tipped in India yellow.

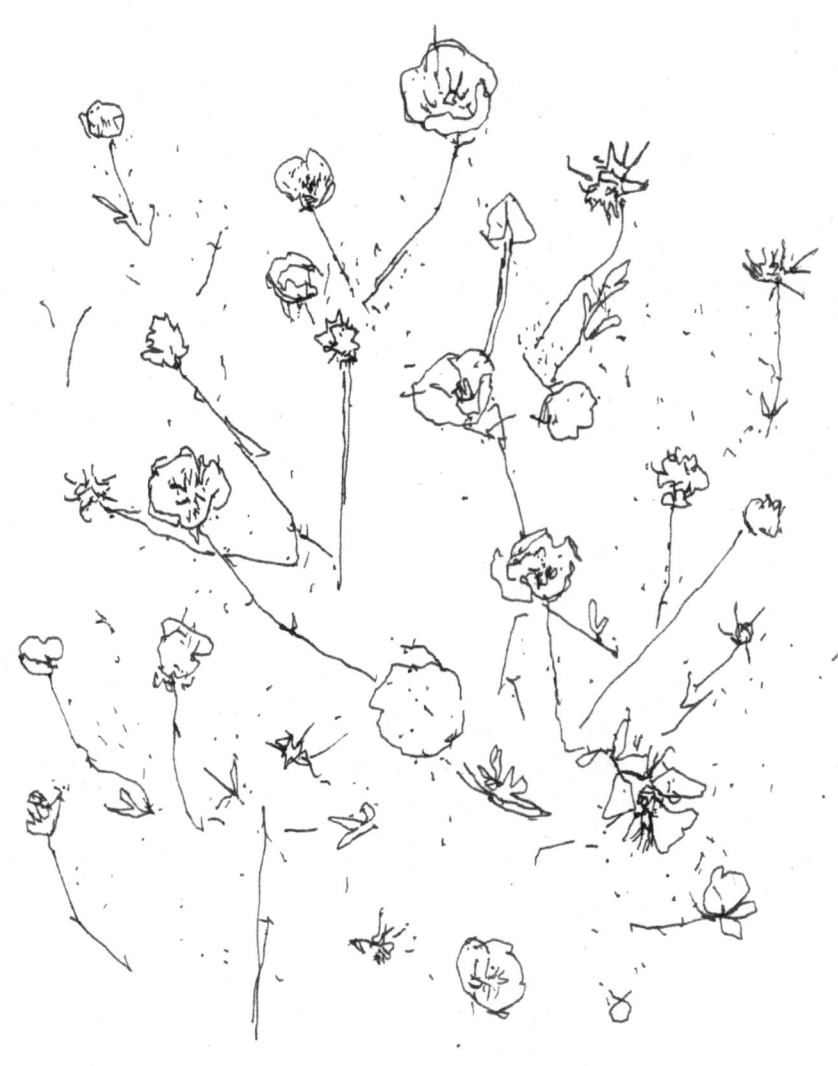

17 July: buttercups (*Ranunculus* spp.)

18 July: perennial sowthistle (*Sonchus arvensis*)

Unbothered here by pedestrians, these plants have grown and spread to their full extent: much taller than those growing through the pavement cracks in town, which have a more taut and meagre aspect. Another richness in variety within the same species.

A lot of plants are going over now. Comfrey stems curl over with the weight of their elongated purple bells. The flowers drop, leaving fine, white spears of pistils in their wake; the foliage bedraggles, twisting into brown. Younger leaves look velvety but their fuzzy surface is scratchy to the touch; their surfaces are blotched with powdery mildew. As they age, the structure of the leaves gets more pronounced, the veins more deeply indented and so darker, shadow-coloured. Patches of rust creep in.

Beneath the indecisive purples of the comfrey is a paler violet cranesbill. Its leaves are reddening at their tips, and some insect or disease is decimating them into lace. Grass seed speckles the surfaces, dropping through the bitten holes like dust. The violet petals are few and far between now, leaving sepals which hold long spikes of seed, the crane's bill of its name.

Further along the railway tracks, cow parsley too has gone to seed, becoming wiry, all its early summer softness forgotten. But acid-flowered ragworts keep on coming up afresh, and tansy brings a warmer yellow hue.

As always, the environment beyond the plant contributes to the marks I make – the passing dog that barks at my odd shape in the grass, the gappy hum of the crickets, the grasses prickling at my shins, the biting of the insects.

21 July

Dandelions in the community centre carpark: fluff-remnants of clocks blowing about the tarmac, bouncing soundlessly about

24 July: spear thistle (*Cirsium vulgare*)

me. I have never seen this movement before. An added benefit of drawing: the excuse to spend some time sitting on the ground.

In adulthood there are few prescribed environments where such a posture is accepted. Beach, playing field, park in summer. Outside of these, you may be regarded with suspicion. I've been reprimanded by security guards or asked to move along when kneeling on the floor of art museums, particularly in New York. Being low to the ground is associated with ducking out or giving up, and ultimately of course with *vagrancy* – a threat to the perceived value of the street. For those concerned with the maintenance of value, this tends to be unnerving if it is seen to happen around those priceless commodities, artworks. Even if those commodities might begin with a person sitting drawing in the grass.

22 July

After several hours planning and packing for a family trip away, my mind is scattered. I head outside for a half-hour in the back garden and find my hands idly reaching out to touch the plants, as if for solace. Goosegrass or cleavers are pulling themselves up through the geraniums, their tacky cling resistant to all but the most determined, carefully gauged tug. The cleavers are flowering now, but almost invisibly – hard to imagine at my scale how those minute blooms, barely a millimetre across, can achieve a reproductive function. At the same time their seeds are forming, fuzzy little pairs of spheres held up in quirky off-shoots from the stem.

I have followed this weed from the very beginning of the year, when it was one of the first to emerge as a soft emerald froth in the pavement cracks. Within weeks it was gathering pace, creeping up tidily at first, threading its rounded stars of leaves tenderly on lax stalks, accelerating in spring, then in a rush rampaging up and through whatever's there, stems stiffening imperceptibly into sticky, ridged wires. Now the cleavers are going to seed it seems to mark a tipping point: the summer's descent. In another month the verges will be shrouded in their cleaving lace.

24 July

We visit family on the other side of the country. I crane my neck as the car slows to see what new plants I might find here, a new housing development with great areas of ground yet to be claimed. Later we head out to buy groceries and, walking back, I stay a while to draw on a quiet residential roundabout. It's the height of summer: so much drama in each square inch of earth.

Spear thistle (*Cirsium vulgare*). The flowers are pinkish mauve and unexpectedly soft, with petals like fine strands of rubber. Scaly bracts hold them upright, relaxing toward the horizontal over time. I'm struggling to register the spiky leaves, their complexity compounded by a propensity to twist. My pen isn't fine enough for the spikes, and I don't get enough sharpness into the drawing. The thistles tower over a foot-high forest of vetch, whose flowers are fading fast to pale mauve. Below this, trifoliate leaves of black medick, a tiny clover, running now to seed.

25 July

A weekend in Wales. The back half of this graveyard has been left unmowed. Flowering grasses fall across the slate headstones, casting shadow portraits somehow more precisely delineated than the flowers themselves. The grasses are up to my chin, swaying gently as if disturbed by the birdsong, and spotted with

25 July: knapweed (*Centaurea nigra*)

great clumps of magenta knapweed (*Centaurea nigra*). This is the stalwart plant that I've been scanning along the edges of the motorway, where it lights the hard shoulder bright purple. It will flower now until the autumn, flourishing in long grass almost anywhere that will let it.

Knapweed's flowers are thistle-shaped: scaly nubs topped by a cerise-pink mohican, but there are no prickles here. Their hairy stems branch stiffly, thickening at the top where they meet the involucre, the whorl of bracts from which the petals emerge. The thickening looks clumsy when I draw it, but an engineer might appreciate the need for width to support those heavy flowers. Knapweed is often known as 'hardheads' – *knop* or *knap* being old words for head – and the heads do feel surprisingly solid; when their petals drop, they harden and darken to black, hence *nigra*.

In Greek mythology, knapweed was named as a flower of the centaurs, since it was used by one of those human-horse hybrids to cure a wound from Hercules' arrow. It has been valued ever since to heal cuts, sores or bruises. Here in the graveyard, it's providing nectar for the circling bees.

I'm drawing to a plaintive cry, a lament of sheep across the valley.

26 July

We have two nights away without the children, much more time than I had anticipated, and I quickly run out of ink. We spend the quiet hours walking, reading, doing very little – but some odd thread between my eye and hand is twitching to draw. Coming home from a river swim, I fill a plastic bag with foxglove petals, pulling them slightly guiltily from each stem. Back inside, I macerate and boil them down to dull maroon, which strained into a mug looks dangerously like herbal tea (foxgloves are highly toxic, containing cardiac glycosides used as a heart stimulant). A poisonous ink suggests intense colour, but the pigment is a disappointingly faint pinkish-grey. When drawn into my pen's ink tank, though, the encrusted remains of black inside darken the flower ink to sufficiency.

The next morning I head out to the foxglove clump at the edge of the carpark. These flower spikes have dropped many of their petals, retaining only a couple of purple trumpets at the tip of each stem. All the rest are forming seeds shaped like tiny pears, each a centimetre in length, topped with a brown stalk as fine as thread. Each seed-pear is held within a star of five green bracts, the top one smaller than the others, like misjudged geometry. A bee is working her way around the stems, entering a trumpet for a few seconds then exiting and hovering mid-air before choosing the next. Is she scenting the quantity of nectar before she makes her choice?

A distant plane exhales into hearing. At the same moment, a pale yellow line I'd thought was a stamen extends itself from the mouth of the flower I'm drawing, stretching into larval life. The plane advances. The caterpillar's exit connects with its sound trail in slow, mysterious precision, moving with equal gravitas. The creature loops its way around the petal's outside to an adjacent leaf, where it comes to a halt, stretched to a line that mirrors the central vein; the plane passes overhead. Both journeys take perhaps half a minute. My nib waits, bee-like, as I watch.

Later in the day I look back at my drawing, finding there the feel of pulling those silky bells from the plant to make its ink. There is something uncanny in their shape; an evocation of our own anatomy, a glove for our digits, as its Latin name, *Digitalis*, bears out. And for the foxes too: a soft covering for slender feet that creep towards their prey – or perhaps away from us, their human hunters.

This sense of the uncanny, of something weirdly familiar in a different species, is made manifest in the Foxglove sculptures of Dorothy Cross, in which the artist picked and cast the foxgloves around her studio, but replaced five bells of each with casts of her own fingers (*Foxgloves*, 2007–2021). The 'lost wax' method of casting ensures the surfaces of skin and flowers are captured in fine detail before translation into bronze. The process 'requires extreme delicacy', Cross has written, and you feel this, the hypersensitivity only a fingertip can feel, looking at their tender, crumpled surfaces, the minute folds and wrinkles preserved forever in the black-green metal.[35] The human digits merge unsettlingly with the plant's, only distinguishable on close looking. A sense of prying human fingers caught and kept.

Part-human and part-vegetal, Cross's *Foxgloves* occupy an uneasy terrain, the place of fear that rises up in dreams or fairytales. And given the plant's toxicity it is an apt anxiety. In the artist's earlier web-based work *Digitalis Purpurea* (2005), a child's voice warns that if you stick your fingers into foxglove flowers and lick them, blindness follows.

28 July

Home. A mizzly morning on the river path. I crouch on a carrier bag in the damp to draw the yellow meadow vetchling scrambling through the grass. A vivid orange bee buzzes among the pea-like flowers, many of which have turned to seedpods, some rattling black, and I'm looking from one stem to another

Dorothy Cross, *Foxgloves*, 2007–2021
(Detail of Foxglove process / petals dipped in wax and finger bell)
© Dorothy Cross, courtesy the artist

to see how the transition happens. It seems the flowers dry and fade, then darken to ragged brown; all the while, the seedpod develops at their centre like a miniature mange-tout, and the brownish tissue of petals falls away. The pod grows larger and blackens as it ripens before splitting open to release its seeds.

The meadow vetchling's leaves are a darker and more glaucous green than its stems. Their structure is invisible in the grass, but if I pull a stem out of hiding I find the twining vetch-like tendrils and winged stalks; their leaves are held ornamentally in neat pairs, a fluid pleasure to draw.

Gulls are calling across the water. An elderly walker I know from this stretch of path passes by. 'Very Turner,' he says with a wink, naturally assuming I'm drawing the river view.

31 July

I make my drawings physically on paper, outdoors, in natural light. But when I want to look at what I've made and assess it in some way, increasingly I find myself scanning it into my computer to view it on the screen – or even snapping a photo of it on my phone, despite the shrinking effect.

My first understanding of this impulse is that it's the framing of the lens or screen that my distracted self is reaching for. After all, we've long framed pictures on our walls, or outlined what's important on a page. A frame defines an area for concentration, sanctioning a temporary disregard for what's beyond, and the screens of our devices add to this a helpful brightness, shine and neat enclosure.

But the digitising reflex seems to go beyond this. I am now so conditioned to analysing and according worth to material presented to me on screen that I have begun to feel unable adequately to assess something unless it's similarly backlit behind glass. It seems the more hours I spend inhabiting online space, the more I need to bring things into that space for them to mean something.

Travel writer Sophy Roberts has observed the way in which, for many of us, the screen has become our dominant terrain, more defining and responsive to the self than the physical places we occupy. 'Our reciprocal relationship with place has been replaced by a digital proxy, of follow and unfollow, of likes and dislikes,' Roberts writes. 'This screen has become "the place" we occupy, seeking validation from the same ancient rhythm of "to know and be known" but without the deeper benefits.'[36] I realise that, even if I don't intend to share a work online, I feel compelled to see *how it would appear* as shareable content. And if a drawing doesn't communicate well via the small bright rectangle of my phone screen, the object itself comes to feel less valuable.*

'Increasingly, the moments of our lives audition for digitisation,' digital commentator Laurence Scott noted in 2015 – already half a lifetime ago in smartphone chronology.[37] A lived experience is now only the first, original incarnation of

---

* Physical artworks and events are now being optimised for screen preconception. The growth of viewing via smartphone, in preference to TV or cinema, is now affecting filmmakers' composing and editing of their shots. Netflix films privilege close-ups and are increasingly unlikely to favour widescreen views in acknowledgement that they'll be less impactful on small mobile devices; artists using Instagram get better responses posting portrait-format images, which get more screen space in the scrolling image feeds. In a recent documentary, set designer Es Devlin admitted she was now designing stadium concerts that work best framed within an Instagrammable square: the experience of being at a Kanye West show in a 10,000-capacity stadium might be a 360-degree one, but it's the flat, two-inch quadrangled smartphone capture that will memorialise it, be most widely seen, and make it count.

itself, and its subsequent appearances may be better lit. To stand a half-hour looking in the grass, facing a small green plant with pen in hand, may offer sufficient immersion to interrupt and elude this digital gravity. But the image that results will likely draw you back into the screen's terrain.

AUGUST

> On mornings when I hope you forget my name,
> I walk through the high wet weeds
> that don't have names either.
>
> Dean Young, 'Selected Recent and New Errors'[38]

In his essay 'The Painter of Modern Life' (1863), Charles Baudelaire vividly described a new kind of figure to be found on the streets of Paris. The *flâneur*, a stroller or wanderer, combined a laconic drifting habit with keen observation of modern life: an ambulatory gaze at once directionless and sharply focused. 'For the perfect *flâneur*, for the passionate spectator, it is an immense joy to set up house in the heart of the multitude, amid the ebb and flow of movement, in the midst of the fugitive and the infinite,' Baudelaire declared.[39] Later, Walter Benjamin would describe the flâneur as one who 'botanizes upon the asphalt'.[40]

During my art school years – my first time living in a city – I became fascinated by the idea of the street as material and spent hours haunting coffee shops with windows overlooking street corners, where I could draw the life flitting past. Kerbstones, bollards, horizontals of parked cars provided fixed lines across which passing bodies registered as a flurry of broken pencil marks, a gait or the set of shoulders all the more compelling for their transience. It's not hard to understand why coffee chains favour corner premises, benefitting from double light and visibility. But the street corner is also place of pause; and this lull, a slowing of pace to wait before crossing a road or considering a change of direction, makes them a flâneur's paradise.

Twenty years later, my walks more often take me out of town to the river, and I'm dropping down to draw on grassy verges more than coffee shop bar stools. I identify now less as flâneuse than migraineuse – one who suffers from chronic migraines.

When I received that diagnosis from a helpful new GP, I enjoyed the feel of the word, with its Parisian flavour of Baudelairian leisure. But in truth the migraineur is the flâneur's opposite. While the latter is drawn to a leisurely stroll amid the noisy bustle of the street, preferably a wide, open boulevard, the former, sensing the arrival of a migraine, seeks urgent cover in a darkened room, with life outside muted or erased by sleep. The flâheuse revels in the cacophony of the city, and records her observations in poetic prose; the migraineuse's heightened sensitivity to light and sound makes her sensation-averse, and often curiously inarticulate, her cognitive abilities tensely abridged. Baudelaire's poetic flâneur is skilfully and evocatively descriptive; I find myself strangely unable, from inside a migraine, to describe how it feels.

AUGUST

I am lucky that, though chronic in their frequency, my headaches are relatively mild, with no accompanying aura. With medication, migraine no longer confines me to a darkened room. And in fact, as long as I have dark glasses, I now find one of the most helpful things I can do to alleviate its symptoms is to go outside.

The therapeutic benefits of being in nature are often spoken of in terms of a reduction of the stress of stimulation. But in a sense the relief of being outdoors, especially among plants, can come not from a lessening of information but rather from its abundance. At the corner of the street, spear thistle draws my fingers to its rubbery purple fringe, offering a tactile microdopamine hit. By the gate at the end of the park I see how cleavers have formed a restraining net that helpfully keeps the nettles back. The movement of long grasses signals to my body how to hold itself, how perhaps to release some tiny tension in my jaw. Identifying these examples is, of course, absurd: countless information is registering on my body through all its senses – sight, scent, sound, taste, touch, proprioception – and the vast majority of it lies beneath my conscious awareness. None of this stuff is for me, none of it requires any conscious response. It is a shimmering flooding of particularity that needn't be named or explained, anticipated or recalled, and vitally, that doesn't bear any pain.

'Clearly, nature calls to something very deep in us,' neurologist and naturalist Oliver Sacks observed. 'The effect of nature's qualities on health are not only spiritual and emotional but physical and neurological. I have no doubt that they reflect deep changes in the brain's physiology, and perhaps even its structure.'* Such structures are mirrored back to us in plants. Look up an image of a neuron: a pyramidal neuron in the cerebral cortex, for example. Its cell body extends into a long straight line with root-like structures at one end, and branch-like dendrites at the top. It looks like nothing so much as the skeleton of a mustard weed I saw this morning.

Those of us who tend to experience the world in an anxious way, which might only mean that we encounter it, at times, in 'too much' detail, may find solace among plants because the environmental detail consumes that capacity, absorbing the mind's hypervigilance.

2 August

Walk home from the library in the descent of a heatwave. The grass is bleaching out; in flowerpots in front of shops the flowers flag; only the weeds remain resilient. We take the long way home, cutting down through the park to the river. Meadow

---

* 'Why We Need Gardens' in *Everything in Its Place: First Loves and Last Tales*, (London: Picador, 2020). A growing body of research investigating the beneficial effects of natural environments on health is explored in Florence Williams, *The Nature Fix: Why Nature Makes Us Happier, Healthier, and More Creative* (New York: W. W. Norton & Company, 2017). Williams describes the *biophilia hypothesis* of Harvard entomologist E. O. Wilson which cites 'the innately emotional affiliation of human beings to other living organisms' – an inevitable effect of our having spent the vast majority of our evolution in nature. Williams also explores the current surge of interest in forest-bathing in Japan, meeting researchers there who have found significant, measurable reductions in heart rate and cortisol levels (both common migraine triggers) in subjects who took walks in the woods. She also meets an immunologist studying the natural killer immune cells which protect us from disease, found to be boosted by 'aromatic volatile substances' such as the turpenes, pinenes and other essential oils emitted by evergreen trees.

buttercups float yellow spots above the flowering grasses. A luminous blue stain of meadow cranesbill.

4 August

Outside the derelict community centre, the stems of rosebay willowherb (*Chamaenerion angustifolium*) are smooth metallic red, almost un-vegetal. This is the flower seen from speeding trains colouring the railway sidings in a magenta haze, or, as here, spreading with fiery rapidity through abandoned lots. A weed of massing quantity, experienced as a population rather than an individual. It's one of many native willowherbs with pink four-petalled flowers, but most of these are soft, diminutive weeds you might crush underfoot; only rosebay grows to human height. Its leaves also bear a peculiar pattern: the veins spread out toward the edge but then loop back before they reach it, each line joining with the next to form a circular network. This distinctive feature can help identify the plant before its flowers come.

A shimmer of swallows makes the sky tremble as I draw. Much smaller movement: a red and black cinnabar moth, working its way up the inflorescence.

Rosebay willowherb is the weed that loves *disturbed ground*, uncanny phrase, that seizes on bombsites, building sites and dereliction. In London during the 1940s it was nicknamed fireweed or bombweed for its habit of appearing in the aftermath of an explosion; its germination can be triggered by heat. By the end of the war it was found growing on 90 per cent of the city's ruins, and described as taking root in London's wounds.[41]

Weeds' survival and flourishing in sites of human destruction presents a powerful image, among the most succinct and famous of which is the Remembrance Day poppy, worn on coat

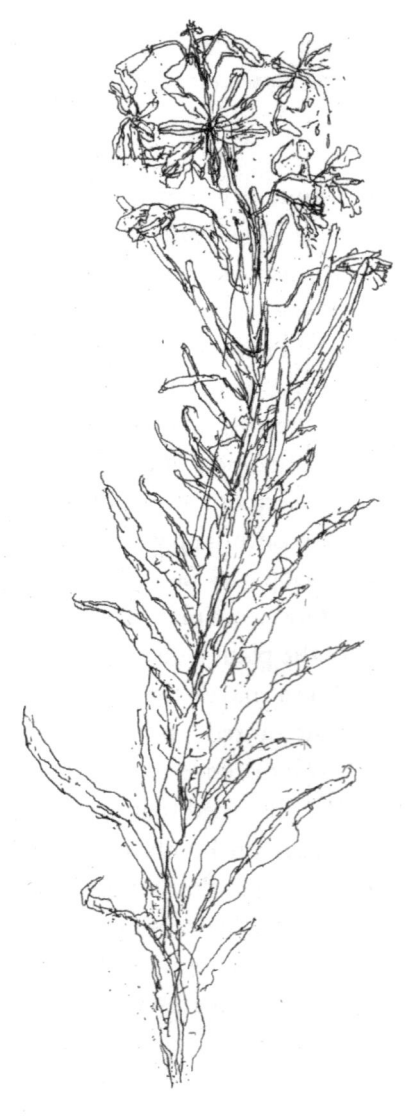

4 August: rosebay willowherb (*Chamerion angustifolium*)

lapels each November. The paper poppy evokes the masses of corn poppies (*Papaver rhoeas*) which germinated in France after the First World War Battle of Ypres, when the excavations of trench warfare exposed long-dormant seeds to the light. And yet other poppies through the ages have been linked, symbolically and pharmaceutically, with the agonising desire to forget. In Greek mythology, the flower is a symbol of Demeter, goddess of agriculture and fertility, who ate its seeds to erase the pain of losing her beloved daughter Persephone, bound to spend half the year in the underworld with her husband, Hades. This was the opium poppy (*Papaver somniferum*), cultivated since the earliest years of human civilisation for its narcotic effects and now farmed for opiate drugs.

In photography, a memorial is made by the fixing of an object on a surface with controlled light. In his series *Addressing the Weeds in Hiroshima* (1997), Portuguese artist João Penalva used an aptly delicate photographic process to capture and memorialise the transience of a cluster of fragile weeds. Like Anna Atkins's cyanotypes, Penalva's images are photograms – images written with light – made by capturing the fall of light around material placed on photosensitive paper. But where Atkins chose each specimen and carefully laid it out, Penalva's weeds are bits of things in motion, strange desperate messages, tangled moments caught unwittingly in a flash of illumination.

When the atomic bomb exploded in Hiroshima on 6 August 1945, the blast effected a devastating flash of its own. Bodies and possessions caught in its path were reduced to objects placed on a light-sensitive surface, leaving horrific shadow residues on the bleached-out concrete.[42] Penalva's process is an echo of the

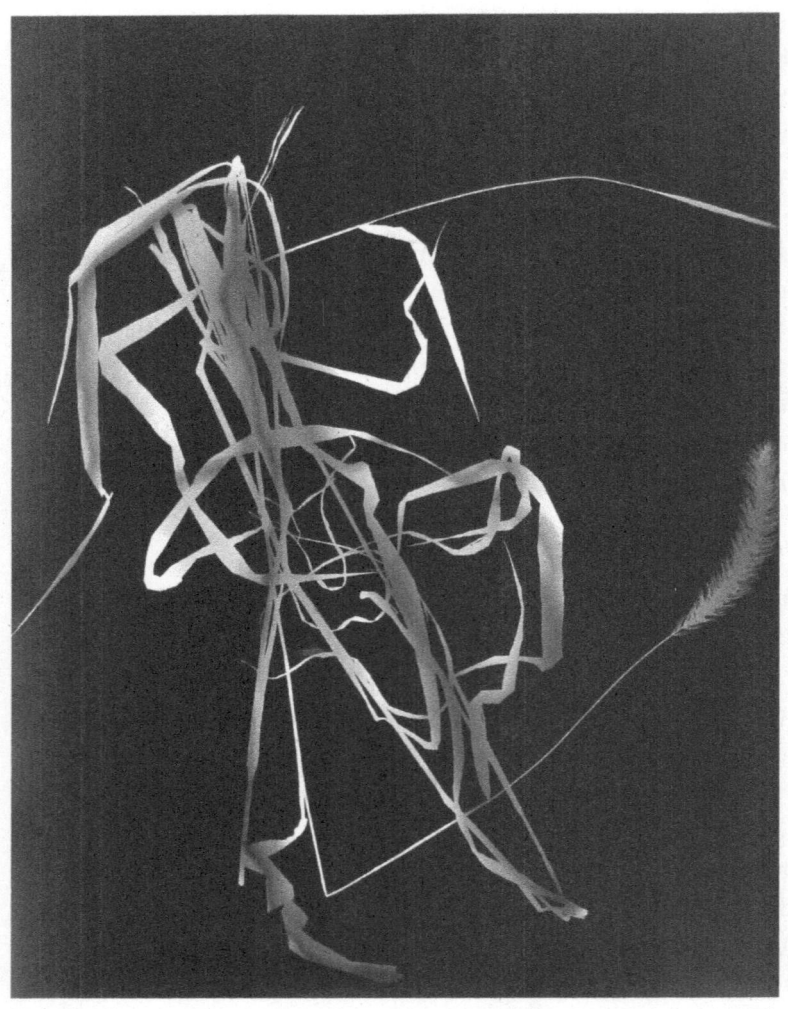

João Penalva, *Caryatia Japonica*, from *Addressing the Weeds in Hiroshima*, 1997
photogram and ink on paper, 59.2 × 44.7cm
© João Penalva, courtesy the artist and Galerie Thomas Schulte, Berlin

blast's, to which his weeds bore witness. The plants he used were taken from the perimeter of a Hiroshima factory used to make army uniforms, a building which on the day of the explosion became an improvised hospital for its casualties.*

The artist had been invited to Hiroshima to take part in a memorial exhibition, *Hiroshima Art Document*. 'Immediately, it caught my eye that the profusion of weeds growing around these buildings and yards had all pushed their way through the asphalt,' he remembered. 'There was no soil to be seen. Their resilience was so striking that I knew they would become my working material.'[43] The weeds Penalva documents enact a living link with what had gone before.

Penalva actually made the images a year after his visit, using a herbarium created for him from the factory's plants. The resilience of weeds makes even tangled blades of grass emblems of survival; but it also reflects something oddly tenuous about them – they are a part of the landscape anyone can take away.

Since discovering Penalva's images, I've started seeing weeds in other conflict zones whenever they are reported, a kind of vegetal gloss on the text of each dispatch. As the current war in Ukraine continues, a friend sends me a newspaper feature on photographers documenting events there.[44] Dima Tolkachov (born 1989) is a Ukrainian photographer who, since the start of the conflict, has focused his lens on its material effects, often finding amid the destruction a bleak and unforeseen beauty. His series *New Grasses* (2022) captures weeds including wild

---

* One of the plants is identified by name as *Setaria faberi*, Japanese bristle-grass – which, in a strange irony, is now a problematic contaminant of grain in North America.

Dima Tolkachov, from *New Grasses*, 2022
digital photograph, 100 x 75cm
© Dima Tolkachov, courtesy the artist

grasses, tree seedlings, a dandelion leaf, sprouting improbably through metal peppered with shrapnel holes. The surfaces around each hole are ripped back like petals. 'I asked myself, "Is the war lasting that long or is the grass growing this fast?"' Tolkachov recalls.[45] The weeds mark out a strange and poignant irony of conflict, their fresh and vigorous growth not only immune to human destruction but finding, like the willowherb on London's bombsites and the poppies in France, new opportunities to thrive. They also express the experience of ongoingness that is invisible and ungraspable to those of us on the outside of the conflict. As Tolkachov writes, 'When studying history, you'll find that each conflict is described with a set of dates, which implies a defined beginning and end. When living through a war, the time seems indistinct, forming a continuous stream. The war was yesterday, it is today, and it will be tomorrow.'[46]

5 August
At the corner of the street, one tiny dove's-foot cranesbill (*Geranium molle*) is growing through a crack in the double yellow line. I've never seen one on this street before. How did it get here? Was its seed dropped by a bird, carried in the sole of a shoe, or blown in on the breeze? So many millions of journeys being made like this, each beginning its own mystery.

12 August
Rosebay willowherb now twice as tall as me and running to seed. Great clusters of rhubarb-coloured, elongated seedpods silently burst open, releasing seeds carried in a weightless fluff of down. The plants are drifting their own layer of cloud across the street.

13 August

Beside the station platform, a perennial sowthistle is up to my chin, magnificent, alive with wasps.

The blackberries are reddening to the colour of a bitten lip. Last weekend I ate ripe berries from a London park, but these northern fruit are way off harvesting. It might not just be the difference in climate, though: I've read there are hundreds of wild blackberry species, with a range of ripening times between them.

The summer seems already to be tiring. Organising our lives through calendars, we see the seasons as divided and successional, even if their transitions may be fuzzy-edged. But the reality in the grass is so much more mutable. You walk ahead, crosscurrents of seasons past and future catching at your sleeve; late frost in June propels you back to spring; new shoots at the end of a year nudge you into the next; dead ragwort stalks from last September persist, half-hidden, in this summer's grass. Today, some sort of wearying and crisping of stem and leaf sends slipstreams of autumn through the air.

15 August

Herb Robert (*Geranium robertianum*) doesn't seem to grow out of the ground as much as appear, hovering, between other things. There's no weight in it, and gravity appears to take no toll on the airy, branching stalks. Its stems are so fine and unemphatic that a single rapid line of my pen is more than enough. Half end in flowers – five small pink petals, requiring only a wavy summary – and half in wispy fruits, fine elongated cranesbills. The flicking, dismissive gesture needed to draw these connects me back to similar movements made when drawing the meadow cranesbill last month: this is muscle memory elucidating a botanical link, for they

15 August: herb Robert (*Geranium robertianum*)

are part of the same *Geranium* family. Herb Robert's ferny leaves are almost childishly outlined, a cartoon version of themselves. For once, instead of looking to complicate, I find I'm aiming for brevity and ease, recording a few scraps of the weed as simply as I can.

Herb Robert generally prefers to grow in shade, and here in the shadow of my garden wall the plant is vivid green. But when it grows in sun its leaves and stalks turn red, a stress response to light. To the medieval eye the reddening stems may have suggested arteries – which then implied the use as a remedy to staunch the blood.

Such linking of a plant's anatomy to the human body and its ailments originated with the ancients. Dioscorides observed, for instance, that 'the Herb Scorpius resembles the tail of the Scorpion, and is good against his biting', and hundreds of other examples are identified in common names.[47] Lungwort (*Pulmonaria officinalis*) has spotted oval leaves which were thought to evoke diseased lungs, while the spore-producing structures on the back of spleenwort's fronds (*Asplenium* ferns) were reminiscent of the spleen. By the medieval period it was believed that God had deliberately created resemblances or 'signatures' in plant forms in order to alert man to their medicinal use. The English botanist William Coles explained in 1657,

> Though Sin and Satan have plunged mankinde into an Ocean of Infirmities, yet the mercy of God which is over all his works, maketh Grass to grow upon the Mountains, and Herbs for use of man, and hath not only stamped upon them a distincte form, but also given particular Signatures, whereby man reade, even in legible characters, the use of them.[48]

And it wasn't only Western medicine. In differing forms, elements of this 'Doctrine of Signatures' can be found in many other traditional medicine cultures across the world.[49] Modern evaluations of the theory have found no evidence that it was plants' morphology that led to medicinal discoveries, and it is much more likely that 'signatures' were post-hoc justifications of what was already believed.[50] But the practice is recognised still for its significant role, in indigenous medicine, as a mnemonic aid.[51] We can't escape our anthropomorphism. Once you've seen a plant's similarity to a part of your body, you don't forget it.

16 August
I'm looking for another kind of wild geranium today: the meadow cranesbill (*Geranium pratense*).* I've come down to the river path to draw them; most of their petals have dropped now, and I don't know how much longer they'll persist so it may be my last chance this summer. But two women on a bench nearby seem to be dissecting the end of a recent love affair, and I'm reluctant to intrude. I stop to look at the plant and begin some tentative, self-conscious preparations, rummaging in my bag for my pen; as the flow of speech continues, I see I'm not disturbing them at all, so it feels OK to drop my bag into the grass and begin.

---

* Many wildflowers' names derive from Greek names of birds, sometimes for surprising reasons. Cranesbill or *Geranium* comes from the Greek *geranos* (crane) because of its beak-like seedcases. Hawkweed or *hieracium* derives from the Greek *hierax*, meaning 'hawk', which was thought to nibble at the plant to improve its sight for hunting. The spurs above *Aquilegia*'s petals evoked the curved neck of an eagle (*aquila*), and celandine was named after the swallow, *chelidon*, whose schedule of arrival and leave-taking seemed to mirror the flowers' own. I learned most of this from Fisher, *The Medieval Flower Book*.

Meadow cranesbill is the most striking of wild geraniums, with its inch-wide violet flowers. I've been glimpsing them through the car window for weeks, blueing the roadside verges and traffic islands. The petals each have five pale veins, neatly drawn as if with a ruler; the petals' edges overlap, doubling the colour, forming a deep purple star.

18 August
I have a morning without my children and decide to head upriver, relishing the prospect of going at my own pace, stopping to draw without interruption or holding anyone back. As I hit the river path, though, I'm drawing a blank. It takes me a bizarrely long moment to realise what's happened – the verges have been cut. In the space of twelve hours, all colour has gone but the greens and beiges of the grasses. The confident pink valerian and the crinkling mallow, acid-yellow ragwort and yolky dandelion, heavy comfrey and diminutive mayweed: all have fallen to the municipal strimmer.

Cutting back is a normal part of maintenance, I know, and in addition to its practical motives – preventing larger plants like comfrey from narrowing the path – it can actually increase biodiversity, opening up the sward. Further along the path the cutting has been less thorough, and I sit down on the verge to absorb the change, and draw a clump of camomile-like mayweed (*Matricaria chamomilla*).* But ten minutes into the drawing footsteps approach, and a pleasant, council-sweatshirted operative is strolling towards me, spraying the severed verges with pesticide. I close my sketchbook and we stop to chat. He tells me he doesn't know why the council are spraying here – he's just

---

* Probably; scentless mayweed (*Tripleurospermum inodorum*) is very similar.

16 August: meadow cranesbill (*Geranium pratense*)

18 August: mayweed (*Matricaria chamomilla*)

following instructions – but thinks they've had complaints about the path becoming overgrown. They try to spray first thing in the morning before the bees are out (though it's now 11am), but he agrees it's the whole ecosystem that will be affected, including the newts he's spotted further up the path.

Why spray? At the time of writing, over eighty councils in the UK have at last banned the use of pesticides, including weedkillers, or at least put measures in place to vastly reduce their use. This might mean focused use to target an invasive species that threatens biodiversity (for example, giant hogweed or Himalayan balsam), or genuine damage to the built environment (Japanese knotweed), or human health (foxgloves in school playgrounds). Developing an effective, pesticide-free weed-management strategy has been shown to be achievable, with techniques including sweeping to reduce the build-up of soil on hard surfaces, planting ground-cover species on areas of bare earth, including around the base of street trees, and using methods like hot foam, which kills plants by exposing them to high temperatures, to target weeds where necessary.[52] Creating an alternative approach may require trials of different methods, and/or investment in new equipment, and so take time; more challenging, perhaps, is shifting the public expectation of how neat and controlled our urban spaces and amenities should look.

Near home, I stop to talk to a neighbour and rest my bag down on the street. A mad tangle of something I've not seen before is racing across the kerb, growing horizontally as if trying to escape. I break a piece off to look it up: common knotgrass (*Polygonum aviculare*). The wiry stems bear tiny dull green leaves and minuscule pink flowers, neat and regular as beads strung on fine lengths of cord.

20 August

At the end of my street an ex-council building has been marked for redevelopment. New fences and chipboard hoardings have gone up, the gate padlocked – and now progress has stalled. But, while human activity is dormant, the tarmacked yard at the back has erupted into life. Peering through the railings I see weeds taller than myself: thistles blowing fluff into the air, spots of golden sowthistle; pink valerian, a line of purple willowherb at the back. Sycamore seedlings punctuate, and there are grasses of all kinds. Below, the usual understorey of nettles, purple toadflax, pellitory-of-the-wall. And over it all a flickering white haze of butterflies.

I sit on a low wall surrounded by parched grass. Here is a late summer dandelion: much taller and meatier than its early season iteration, the polite, soft spears Anna Atkins recorded; it now takes on more wayward shapes, a burnt-out office worker going rogue. Its stems twist out of verticals, contorted by stress or drought or perhaps just the weight of the flowers.

I start to draw a flowerhead, still loosely closed this early in the morning, then move on to the stems and leaves below. By the time my nib returns to add more detail to the clenched flower it has opened in the sun and now presents a tousled yellow disc. What to do? I can either make up the information as it was, using another flower and memory to supply the missing lines, or I can reassess, adding in the new outline I see. If I want my drawing to remain in the present, I have to do the latter. Sometimes a 'mistake' is a truthful record of change.

24 August

Back in the woods, autumn is coming like a hand passing over a face. Very few campions still hold their petals. I've stopped at

21 August: dandelion (*Taraxacum* spp.)

a mossy stump. Minute pine needles dash the earth in burnt umber. Among them, naive green is pushing through in pairs of leaves. I don't know what they are but draw them anyway.

Upriver, Himalayan balsam (*Impatiens glandulifera*) has taken over. Our walk takes twice the normal time as the children stop to set off every seedpod, the swollen ribs of 'policeman's helmets' exploding at the slightest touch. The plant's reaction is so quick it confuses chronology, apparently happening a moment before contact. The detonated remnants show spring-loaded coils, uncannily mechanical.

The balsam here, as on many other UK riversides, is considered invasive. I'm feeling uneasy that our game is furthering its spread, but they can be detonated even by a raindrop and hardly need our touch. The plant was a Victorian introduction to the UK – the classic tale of a plant collector bringing back a new exotic flower, with no idea how it might spread or what impact it would have on native species. Balsam can grow three metres in a summer, outpacing and outshading everything else. Its fragrance, too, dominates the path; a strange resiny scent that seems almost synthetic.

29 August

Whether it's back-to-school feeling we never quite shake off, or just the sensation of the season's turn, the end of August always seems a particularly evocative time: warm breezes and the first leaf-fall recalling previous summers' ends.

Last August, pushing my grandmother's wheelchair along the paved paths of her care home garden, my mother and I picked odd stems and placed them in her lap: yarrow, mint, lavender, crushing them a little to release their scent into her still hands. A hundred years old, she was receding now over increasing distances, dropping into sleep or remote terrains of memory for growing stretches of time, and I missed her and wanted her with me, sharing the same sights and scents I was experiencing in the late summer garden. It was only a handful of years since she had helped me plant up my first garden, tapping the young perennials out of their pots and coaxing out their roots with gentle, gnarled fingers.* Yet, while she receded from the present we both occupied, my grandmother didn't seem to be receding from herself, but rather travelling more deeply into herself, into her own history. When she greeted me or listened to my news, she seemed to come up to meet the present from the depths of that self, bringing into her response some intangible experience from each of her ten decades of life.

My grandmother was losing her short-term memory, and a little of her long-term understanding as well. 'I have holes in my head,' she would say. She sometimes seemed untethered from current events, even at the local level of her own room; it was as if the ties that bind us to our currency had come loose and her boat was drifting out, with the rope lying only lightly curled around its mooring. Yet in her handling of plants, in her greeting of my face at the window, in almost all of our encounters I felt her to be more *there* than I was. To understand 'being present' only through its use of tense, only as being aware of what is happening right now, seems a depletion both of its meaning and our own.

---

* My grandmother was quite well then, but, fascinatingly, Oliver Sacks observed that even patients of his with very advanced dementia, disorientated and unable to tie shoelaces or handle simple tools, retained an instinctive ability to handle plants. 'Put them in front of a flower bed with some seedlings, and they will know exactly what to do – I have never seen a patient plant something upside down.' Sacks, 'Why We Need Gardens', 245.

My own short-term memory functions just fine, and I occupy my body with relative ease, but it's not where I reside most of the time. Aren't you the same? Vast swathes of our waking hours are spent on the lookout for something or somewhere else, even while ostensibly we're busily occupied. Unconscious either of the intention or its object, I'll find myself searching through the vertical frame of my phone, the horizontal desktop screen, or in the pages of books, or out of windows. And I can hardly blame technology. The philosopher Blaise Pascal identified 'man's inability to sit quietly in a room alone' four centuries before a digital world could even have been imagined, let alone scapegoated.[53] Most days it seems the incessant searching only resolves itself at night, as we finally manage to elude ourselves in sleep.

Is this why I seize on drawing and writing – to account for myself? Am I reaching for lines and words simply to lay claim to having witnessed something, to having something to report? Are my words and drawings, is all writing and drawing, a kind of reverse alibi: a scrawled rebuttal of absence?

29 August: yarrow (*Achillea millefolium*)

SEPTEMBER

> I bequeath myself to the dirt to
> grow from the grass I love,
> If you want me again look for
> me under your boot-soles.
>
> Walt Whitman, 'Song of Myself', *Leaves of Grass*[54]

1 September

Early in the evening, just as the light is turning warmer and sadder – the kind of light that makes you narrow your eyes and remember – I walk up to the park behind the train station to draw. The gardener in charge of the town's parks has taken a swathe of its margin here to sow wildflowers and it's become a meadow in miniature. I sit among grasses tall as my chest, interspersed with flowers that were once a common sight in English fields, and are now more often confined to quaint *Observer's* guides: cornflowers, corn cockle, poppies, yellow rattle. Tallest among them, and my favourite, are the ox-eye daisies.*

---

* Happily, the ox-eye daisy is more resilient than many cornfield flora. Richard Mabey observes in *Flora Britannica* that that it will readily colonise grassy areas left unsprayed. Having been eliminated from much farmed grassland it

Leucanthemum vulgare is the largest of the wild daisies, and its yellow-domed centre is so intensely rich in pollen that you'll often see smudges of the colour dusted across its petals. In a study of sixty-five different British meadow flowers, the ox-eye daisy scored the highest for quantity of pollen and nectar.[55] Its stems are surprisingly wiry and bend eccentrically, tilting the flowers askew, so that the mass effect is of a curious listening crowd.

Like other white flowers, the ox-eye's petals seem to glow in darkness or low light – a means of attracting crepuscular insects – and this explains its other common name of moon flower. Perhaps the lunar evocation brought about its link, historically, with divination. In France it was used in romantic predictions, a custom which endures in the traditional game she loves me, she loves me not, thought to have originated with these daisies. In parts of Austria and Germany the plant was hung on roofs and doors for protection against lightning.

Here at the edge of the park the moon flowers are on the wane; many have lost their petals, their centres turning brown and held at angles increasingly acute. The evening light rakes through the leaves and stems, creating new lines from their intersection, dissolving boundaries, fusing it all together. I abandon any intention of singling out the daisies in my drawing, and simply try to register as many lines as I am able.

is now increasingly common in set-aside areas and common verges. Richard Mabey, *Flora Britannica* (Chatto & Windus / Sinclair Stevenson, 1996), 373. It also makes a brilliant garden flower. I threw a handful of its seeds on an unused bit of earth years ago, and the flowers come back reliably each year, without spreading further than they are welcome. For more on weeds that work well in domestic gardens see Jack Wallington, *Wild About Weeds: Garden Design with Rebel Plants* (London: Laurence King Publishing, 2019).

As I walk back down the street, the streetlamps flickering on, I consider what I'll tell the others of what I've seen. After all, there are risks in declaring something beautiful. Is it that calling attention to beauty claims its space somehow, depriving others of a foothold? I am wary of sharing such impressions with my children, since from a parent this can easily come across as an encouragement to appreciate, which will often elicit the opposite response. Appreciation tends to need to steal in, like scent.

But it's not only that. There is a certain privacy, perhaps even a secrecy about the experience of beauty which can fade out in the exposure of communication, like opening the back of an analogue camera and bleaching the film. Such experiences, as philosopher and ecologist Timothy Morton has written, often rely on a sense of not-knowing-why; of bafflement, even: 'I can't isolate it without ruining what precisely is beautiful about it.'[56]

Near the beginning of *Bluets*, her ode to that most elusive colour, Maggie Nelson refers to something similar when she warns, 'please do not write to tell me about any more beautiful blue things'. She promises the reader, 'This book will not tell you about any, either. It will not say, *Isn't X beautiful?* Such demands are murderous to beauty.'[57]

Does the creation of an image offer an alternative? A drawing avoids gasped platitudes, maybe, but it is equally susceptible to cliché. The eye falls gratefully on well-rehearsed formulas of shape and line as eagerly as the tongue. Particularly when drawing more celebrated wildflowers, whose familiar forms can't help but evoke countless previous representations, making it harder to respond with clarity and a fresh eye.

One thing a drawing can do, potentially at least, is attest to a period of time spent concentrating on its subject. Lines take

1 September: meadow with ox-eye daisies (*Leucanthemum vulgare*)

the time they take to draw; end to end they measure out inked distances drawn at the speed the body needs and understands: physically and without words. Perhaps this durational evidence has a certain worth of its own, a testimony that can stand in silent stead of comment, caption, exclamation.

In her novel *Second Place*, Rachel Cusk describes a sense of artworks as free space, a territory unclaimed by language. 'There's something that paintings and other created objects can do to give you some relief,' her character observes. 'They give you a location, a place to be, when the rest of the time the space has been taken up because the criticism got there first.'[58]

3 September

In the cracks between the concrete paving at the back of the house, a small green weed is blurring the straight lines. I don't know the plant and turn to my favourite botanical guide, Roger Phillips's *Wildflowers*, to look it up.[59] Petty spurge (*Euphorbia peplus*) – ironically, a relative of the euphorbias I've bought and planted in the flowerbed nearby. *Petty* is a predictably derogatory adjective for a weed; *spurge* indicates a plant with milky sap. This is good to know, since the sap can irritate the skin when it leaks from picked stems. I don't need to pick this plant though; I grab an old tin flowerpot to perch on and begin to draw.

Phillips's guide is so helpful to the novice reader because it was written by a photographer rather than a botanist, who understands not only the information you want to know but how to help you find it. How much more useful, to those of us without botanical training, to organise his book not by genus or family, but in chronological order of flowering. Each plant is captioned with the date on which it was photographed: consult the book by turning to that portion of the year. Even if you don't find what you're looking for, you'll come across other plants in flower now that you can look out for.

The other thing I love about Phillips's approach is his rejection of the usual emphasis of botanical illustration on an 'average specimen', which, though it specialises in bringing out the salient features of a plant, can somehow estrange us from reality. Plants in the wild never seem to be salient examples of themselves. 'My specimens are not idealized versions but normal ones in the typical condition that you might find them,' Phillips writes in his introduction. It is the small irregularities and imperfections, the oddly twisted leaf, misshapen petal, curling stem, that make the plants more recognisable.

6 September
Along the river path, the mallows have gone to seed almost entirely now, only a few scraps of pink clinging on. Tansy is browning over like scorched cake. Many others – the geraniums, thistles, umbellifers and purple deadnettles – are fading away into a background warp and weft of brittle stalks. But comfrey is coming up afresh. It's one of the flowers I missed out on drawing earlier in the summer, so I'm glad to have another chance to draw it while my family pick blackberries along the path.

As I follow the stalk down with my pen, I'm trying to work in a sense of its hairy texture, and the movements I need to do this – quick minuscule jerks that force me to hold my breath – trigger a memory of drawing green alkanet earlier in the year. Thanks to these movements, I realise the texture of the stems is similar, and when I look the plants up later I find they are in the same family – *Boraginaceae* (the group includes borage, another noticeably hirsute example). This is a piece of knowledge I could simply have read in a wildflower guide, but, had I only done that, the fact would have meant little. It was the physical feeling of trying to draw the prickly texture of their stems that led me to intuit their connection, just as the flicking gesture of registering a cranesbill seedhead did back in July.

A huge amount of information arrives like this, in what can be understood as embodied cognition or whole-body thinking.* Our observations don't take place in disembodied heads. Struggling to find a clear patch of ground in a field to kneel and draw a spear thistle shows me how densely and prolifically they self-seed. I measure the height of a species in relation to my own body when I stand facing it with the sun in my eyes or, crouching down, get cramp in my foot in the effort of seeing it more clearly. If I'm struggling to get the indentation down the centre of a petal fine enough, the tension in my hand tells me it's a particularly narrow crease.

This kind of sensate knowing feels different to verbal information; I believe it differently because it's backed up by my body, and this in turn makes it significantly more memorable. Its usefulness is felt rather than told, and even without further botanical context it feels meaningful because it relates to how I experience and move through my environment.

---

* Embodied or distributed cognition refers to the understanding that rational cognition – the thinking that takes place in our cortices – is significantly influenced by our bodies. My understanding of its theories was shaped by the many speakers at 'The Extended Mind', a conference organised by Talbot Rice Gallery at the University of Edinburgh in conjunction with its exhibition of the same name, 2019.

6 September: comfrey (*Symphytum officinale*)

'We have come increasingly to forget that our minds are shaped by the bodily experience of being in the world,' observes Robert McFarlane in his introduction to *The Living Mountain*, Nan Shepherd's profoundly sensorial study of the Cairngorm landscape. 'We are literally losing touch, becoming disembodied, more than in any previous historical period.'[60] As increasing proportions of learning and teaching occur online, in virtual spaces which have the benefit of greater accessibility and reach, I can't help thinking about the loss of imprint on the body and, consequently, its impoverished contribution.

12 September
We walk along a new path further upriver, out of sight of town. The first leaves have fallen and the browns are taking over. Branches of the willows hugging the riverbank are twisting into yellow; mustard-coloured lichens fur their trunks. Campion has long gone to seed, and a light breeze brings an almost weightless rattle from its papery husks. Hogweed skeletons star-spangle the path. On the lusher side that drops down to the water, St John's wort is lighting up the grass.

The stems of summer's flowers are fading out now, drying, growing brittle. In the shadier stretches, hordes of rosebay willowherb scribble crazed half-circles with their fluffy seed. Biscuit-coloured grasses zigzag through everything, falling over themselves. Sentinels of dock punctuate with deep rust.

There is freshness too, though: glossy blackberries dot the brambles' arching chaos, a perfect spot of light on every drupelet; occasional ragworts persevere, and pink herb Robert flowers revel in the shady depths.

12 September: campion seedheads (*Silene dioica*)

14 September

I've been putting off drawing ragwort (*Jacobaea vulgaris*, or *Senecio jacobaea*), and assumed my unconscious aversion to the plant was due to its reputation as a toxic nuisance. Ragwort is well-known as poisonous to cattle, and, though its bitter taste means grazing livestock instinctively avoid it, it can harm them if the cut and dried plants get mixed up with their feed. Visually, there's a harshness about its striking acrid yellow; it doesn't seem to blend easily with other wildflowers but stands stiffly apart. A tough plant, it's also difficult to uproot.

And, as it turns out, the plant is also really awkward to draw. As I start trying to map it out on the page I hear my mind complaining that there's just too much of it. The flowers seem congested, cramped together: even a single young stem can bear twenty, forty, sixty of them, scruffy clumps of buds as well as the open daisies. The plants stand in rigid triangles that lie awkwardly on the page.

I make two drawings: the first focusing on a single stalk, the second faster, taking in a broader sweep. Upping the pace makes it harder – I'm working at the edge of my ability, moving the pen slightly ahead of what my brain can oversee, as if my hand is a child that's running just too far ahead. But, though it reduces control, in an odd way this method can result in greater accuracy, since it's impossible to reflect too much or to fall back on any judgments of how the drawing is going. I'm drawing too fast for interference.

As I struggle with the spacing of the buds around the stem, trying to accommodate them all, I am impressed despite myself. The plant is really packing its flowers in, maximising its chances and its offering to insects, too. Later I learn it's one of the UK's

14 September: ragwort (*Jacobaea vulgaris*)

Albrecht Dürer, *Great Piece of Turf*, 1503
watercolour, pen and ink on paper, 40.3 x 31.1cm
Albertina, Vienna

top ten plants for nectar production and is the sole food source for at least thirty insect species, seven of which are officially deemed scarce.[61]

Ragwort's generic name *Senecio* means 'old man', a nod to its fluffy white seedheads. Its common names tend to be derogatory: rag because of the ragged-looking leaves; stinking Billy or mare's fart due to its unpleasant smell when bruised. Maybe ragwort will always be an outlier, holding itself apart, but for what it gives to invertebrates, at the very least, it's a plant worthy of respect.

18 September

I didn't realise how many plants had late flushes. Mounds of herb Robert, nettles, yarrow and cleavers are springing up along the parched verge edges. Low-raking sun illuminates silver snail trails on the asphalt. Dandelions have lost their clocks.

21 September

An occasional game I play at this time of year, when the grasses are in flower, is to search for a certain five-hundred-year-old scrap of turf. An ordinary patch of grasses and weeds, dandelions, plantain, yarrow, maybe if I'm really lucky a stem or two of burnet saxifrage. The patch I'm looking for is the *Great Piece of Turf* painted by Albrecht Dürer in 1503.

The watercolour itself is in the Albertina museum in Vienna and I've never seen it in person, but a postcard of this favourite painting has kept me company above my desk for years, a kind of talisman. It's generally reckoned to be the first realistic depiction of plants in Western art.

Where medieval herbals show plants as if placed flat upon a tabletop and viewed from above, Dürer's viewpoint is from down in the grass, ground level – even if, pragmatically, he likely took the chunk of turf into his studio. Each plant seems to be drawn as it is at a particular moment, on a particular day; a world apart from the stylised renderings in the *Circa Instans*, two centuries before. And each is interwoven with the next: an ecosystem in miniature.

Like his contemporaries, Dürer mainly painted religious narratives – the Church being the most important patron of the time – and his treatment of plants in these paintings develops over years. In an early picture, *St Jerome*, painted around 1495, eight years before the *Great Piece of Turf*, Dürer includes weeds in the foreground in a fairly cursory way. The brushstrokes show he's enjoying the flourishy curves and highlights on them, but they're not serious plants – they are close to ornament. Whorls of something a bit like dandelion has leaves that are closer to those of an oak, with rounded tips; beyond a few ears of wheat and possibly some sort of woundwort, I can't identify any of the plants with certainty. Within a decade, though, in the foreground of *The Adoration of the Magi* (1504) there's a clearly defined and recognisable plantain. By 1508, in *The Martyrdom of the Ten Thousand*, the foliage being trampled by falling bodies is as clear and real as the weeds at the end of my street.

By this point, Dürer probably didn't need to take those weeds into his studio to study. Thousands of hours of direct observation over the past two decades, not least the *Great Piece of Turf*, are stored within him. Dürer valued what he termed 'copying' from nature so highly that he referred to this accumulated experience of looking as 'the stored-up treasure of the heart':

> no one can ever achieve a beautiful picture from out of his own sense perceptions, unless by much faithful copying he has stocked his mind full [...] Out of that, the stored-up secret treasure of the heart becomes manifest.[62]

I'm curious about the inclusion of 'secret', which seems to connect to that sense of privacy in the experience of beauty mentioned above. Dürer goes on to caution that we should never rest on our preconceptions, but should continue to look afresh:

> whoever has achieved good practice out of proper understanding has the potential to make something good without any object to copy, so far as ability permits. Yet it will always become better, if all his life he practises copying [from nature].[63]

To judge from the intimately observed study of cowslips he made two years before his death, Dürer clearly followed his own advice. Perhaps this reverence for nature, rooted in his religious convictions, helps to explain his focus on specificity. If I look at a plant drawing by a contemporary of his, such as any of Leonardo's flower studies, I see a honing-down to the essential shapes: sheets of flowers turn this way and that, working out archetypes of themselves. Stems and stamens curve smoothly; leaf and flower forms tend to the generic; many of them seem to be auditioning to be carved in stone on a pillar. Leonardo reaches for perfection of type. His plants are never vulnerable. Dürer on the other hand is all about the particular: about fidelity to this particular flower growing in these specific circumstances. When he draws and tints that tuft of cowslips, it's not even a pure specimen: wisps of grass have got in, and a bit of clover threads its way right through the centre.

It is likely that the *Great Piece of Turf* was considered as a preparatory study, a work intended to furnish details for a larger religious narrative, but I like to think such diligence was also a pretext.* Unlike many of his smaller botanical studies, this painting feels like an end in itself: an experiment, perhaps, in how far can you go with how little; a distant foreshadowing of Perec's question, 'What Happens when Nothing Happens?'

As I walk up to my children's school, half looking out, again, for Dürer's turf, I wonder what it is about this painting that makes it so enduringly fascinating. It is more than the shock of finding something so acutely relatable from half a millennium ago, striking though that is. A drawing or painting records the time of its making, distils that time, and holds it apart. If an ancient image shows us something that seems very present, something so intimately familiar that we might find it if we step outside right now, it can offer a route through the particular towards such timelessness.

There are things we know but keep on needing to be shown. I know that such clusters of weeds and grass are coming up as they did five hundred years ago, right now, outside, and I can even believe that, pesticides notwithstanding, most will continue. But to see an image of such continuance is assuring on some deeply felt, non-intellectual level. And beyond this, beyond the continuance of the plants I crave being shown, is the

---

* Several other botanical studies in watercolour survive, including a smaller piece of turf with columbine and one eerily modern sheet of eight wildflowers.

continuance of witness. Because Dürer is only looking at weeds, and nothing else is happening, the painting becomes as close as such an artwork might be able to get to a picture of nothing. The witnessing becomes something strangely pure, curiously visible. This is a painting of a patch of weeds, but, in another sense, it is a painting of a fellow human looking: a painting of attention.

24 September

A flush of growth is coming through the gravel near the front door, the new plants easier to make out without the cover of grass. Fresh dandelions, sowthistle, coltsfoot, the ever-present small-flower hairy willowherb (*Epilobium parviflorum*). One of the most diminutive weeds is a hairy bittercress (*Cardamine hirsuta*) that has gone to seed. Its seedpods are surprisingly pronounced: elongated with a throwaway tip, like those of a cranesbill. The whole plant is barely a couple of inches tall and the stems near the top are as fine as the lightest drawn line I can achieve by using my nib upside down.* I get as close as I can to draw, but still I'm at the limit of my vision, barely able to make out which line of stalk branches off from which. The added difficulty this brings helps me focus more strongly; it seems to give the drawing a peering quality.

Quite quickly I become aware of an unfamiliar swish, a light movement happening every half second or so, and realise

---

* Writing this reminds me of the 'certain Chinese encyclopedia' of Jorge Luis Borges, whose vividly anthropocentric animal classifications included such definitions as '(k) drawn with a very fine camelhair brush, (l) et cetera, (m) having just broken the water pitcher, (n) that from a long way off look like flies'. (My own might be 'those small and slight enough to require a nib used upside down'.) The encyclopedia is quoted by Michel Foucault in *The Order of Things: An Archaeology of the Human Sciences*, translated by Alan Sheridan (London: Routledge, 2001).

24 September: hairy bittercress (*Cardamine hirsuta*)

it's me: I'm wearing my winter coat for the first time and my head turning against the collar, as I swivel my gaze back and forth between plant and page, is sounding a soft fabric alert. The sound shows me a rhythm of my body drawing that I hadn't known before.

I pause halfway as the smallest amount of rain appears on the paper, rain so light it seems not to have fallen but rather manifested on the page.

27 September

Sometimes lush grass on a downward slope calls out to the body before the brain can interfere. The children and I have reached the summit of the hill and before I know what's happening I've dropped my bag and sunk into the turf. My children, always ahead of the game when it comes to physical instinct, have flung off their coats and are on their bellies, rolling down it. They are shrieking with delight then crying out that they feel sick then back to delight again. Halfway down, my daughter gets up and runs the last stretch down to the lake, calling out at the top of her voice 'I'm ALIVE!'

I get out my notebook and look about at the ground. No plants are rising above the grass's surface – this is mown lawn – but of course there are still weeds here. Within the sward I find minute yarrow, clover, self-heal, daisies; none of them raising flowers above the blades but all interrupting its texture at the level of close detail. Each gives me a pinpoint in the chaos, a reference point for my eye as I begin to draw. Without the weeds I'd be lost in uniformity.

Even with the weed markers, drawing this patch of ground still feels like sitting with the impossible. But there is, paradoxically, a kind of restfulness in that. No pressure when there's nothing to achieve or fix. If it were approached with some objective standard of representation, drawing a square foot or two of grass in the time I have (maybe half an hour, depending on weather, the mood of the children and our growing hunger) would be an absurd task. I could only really capture a few centimetres in that time with any notion of accuracy. Instead, what I'm asking of myself is a kind of non-asking; I'm drawing not with the intention to depict what I see, but as a way of simply staying with it. My pen starts moving with a relaxed sense of hopelessness but as the rhythm of looking and marking builds momentum I find a haphazard approach. The weeds in the grass help tether me, acting as fixed points around which to move my gaze. I'm making marks quickly, unconcernedly, in a mixture of specific reporting – outlining certain particularly pronounced blades of grass – approximation – inserting small patches of directional lines – and a hovering, transitional flurry between the two.

This is drawing as a process of staying longer. I carry the feeling of this patch of grass, this patch of time with me into the evening. It is a deep, non-verbal sense of *I was there.*

27 September: weeds in lawn

OCTOBER

> Your skin is more than skin. It is at
> the same time an enormous leaf,
> in which your whole body is wrapped ...
>
> Eduardo Navarro and Michael Marder,
> 'Vegetal Transmutation'[64]

1 October

I'm writing this from the corner table of a supermarket café, in a retail park just out of town. It's the kind of location anthropologist Marc Augé might have described as a *non-place*, when he wrote, in the early 1990s, of those increasingly ubiquitous places of supermodernity – airports, motorways, hypermarkets – that intentionally lack their own identity, individuality or relation to historical place. Though the café itself is average-sized, when I look up to the roof it is hundreds of feet above me in the remote dark of an industrial warehouse. In place of windows, the café's views are images of menu items, photographed in absurdly flattering light, and the air conditioning produces an almost anaesthetically lulling hum. Yet even somewhere as generic as this, where every message, product and surface has been

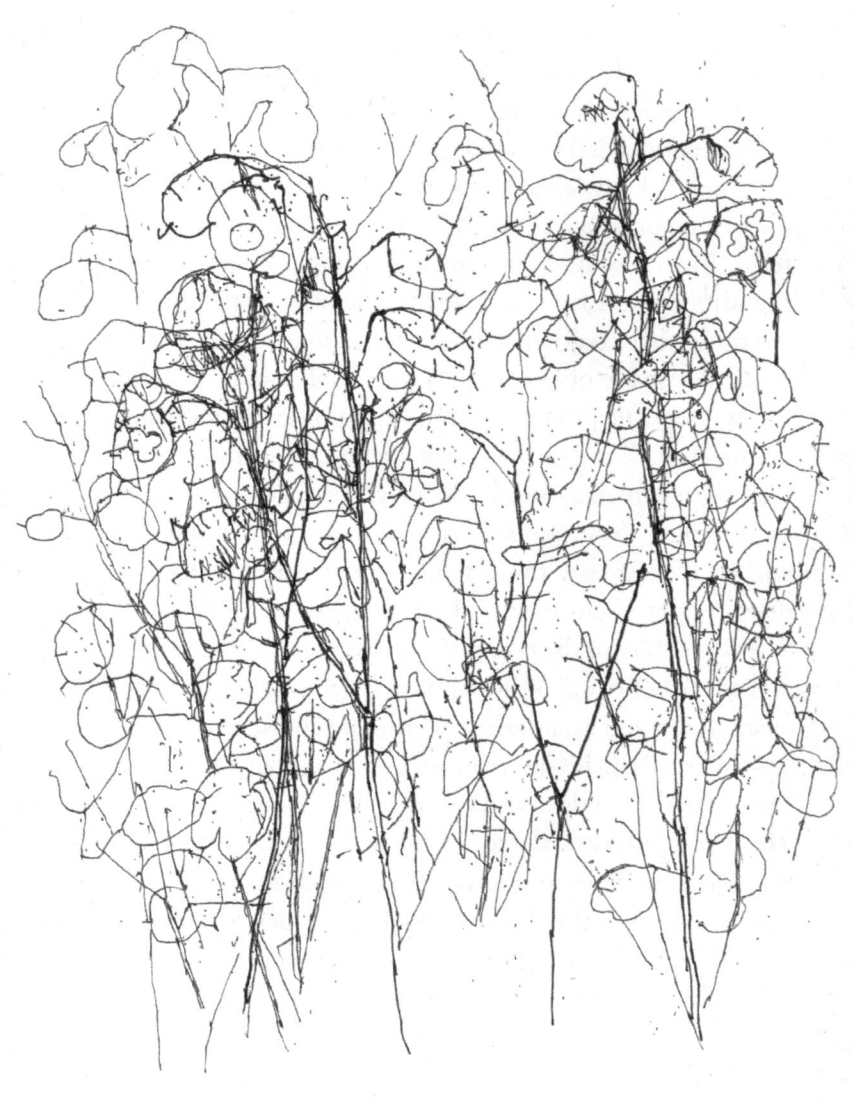

1 October: honesty seedheads (*Lunaria annua*)

regulated in some central office, the individual creeps in. As I sip my coffee I see signs of regular customers, greeted warmly with extensive chat, and favoured tables among the uniform rows; seats avoided too, or marked by scuffs or splits in the vinyl.

Augé acknowledged that the idea of a non-place was not something pure, but in practice would always constitute a relative term. Even the most functional and impersonal of venues, like the airport corridor that takes you to your plane and excludes anything that could encourage you to linger, will have its own particular shade of lighting, its own timbre of air conditioning, its own acoustic properties of industrial flooring and wipe-clean paint. And, however hardwearing, those surfaces will accrue identifying marks: odd stains or chips that a regular traveller might come to recognise, consciously or not. A flight of steps will wear unevenly toward the centre; the handles on swing doors might show the subtle dominance of right-handedness. The anonymity of the non-place is always under threat from wear and tear, the patina of living; just as, outside, its perimeter will crack or dip and accumulate debris; and so the weeds will come.

I drive back home along the A-road that loops round the town. Along its edges and central reservation, weeds flash past. There's something staggering about the way they hold their own that seems to defy the game of time and distance. To the driver, the motorway is the ultimate non-place, merely a standardised conduit between one destination and the next. But the weeds refute that. Their presence claims every inch of it as *location*.

2 October

Just past the equinox; the beginning of autumn. I feel a pang on noting the new month on my phone screen; I've internalised a haphazard calendar of flowering times and almost everything tails off in September. My reading brain tells me it's all over but heading out, it's a different story. Fresh crops of nettles and cleavers are coming up along the path where the council sprayed. We've not had a frost yet and the plants are still shoulder-to-shoulder with me, just darkening. Umbellifers, grasses, thistles, dock and fireweed are all stiffening as they run to seed: desaturated, yet more firmly present than in their flowering prime.

A triangle of waste ground borders the council playpark. Rooks cawing, faint cries of children on the swings; a light breeze. Sharp tang of a bonfire from the allotments over the hill. I come off the path into the wild tangle of weeds. My feet are held in a bed of ivy so dense I make a mental note not to drop my pen as I'm sure I'd never find it again. Waist deep in honesty. Pearly moon-discs are held in the finest lead-wire frames. Their seeds are placed neatly on the perpendicular, blurrily visible on small ruled lines. For the first time since the spring my paper feels cold to the touch; I break off to rub the side of my drawing hand warm and flex my fingers.

A few minutes into the drawing my foot goes numb; I adjust my body and my perspective changes, shifting the information that I'm dealing with, necessitating a renegotiation. A drawing made from life will always register a struggle of this kind; an effort above all to connect.

To draw, instead, from a photograph is to regard an image that refuses to change. However I move my body or gaze as I draw, a photograph gives me the same information; it won't reveal anything new. This makes the work of drawing easier, but something is lost. The effort to connect is not the same.

6 October: purple toadflax (*Linaria purpurea*)

3 October

I've completely changed my mind about the ragwort now that it's gone to seed. The colours are mellowing exquisitely: soft, copper-brown spent flower bracts resemble tiny suns. It's a reminder that the image of a plant held in the mind's eye doesn't need to be its flowering peak.

5 October

Drew comfrey in the woods this morning while my children ran off to hide. After a while my son darted back and, seeing what I was doing, placed himself solidly on the exact spot of ground I was drawing. As I shifted my focus, he moved too, and it became a game. He was placing himself in the beam of my attention. I have found that children can often sense attention even when it's not in view, as if magnetised, perhaps drawn by the particular still quiet of watching. After a minute we ran on to join the others.

6 October

Early evening, nipping out to draw while the dinner cooks. Purple toadflax (*Linaria purpurea*), immediately after rain. Fat droplets bulge the outlines of each stem and leaf. The plant is leaning heavily, or is that me – both of us seem to have the posture of a last ditch attempt. Fatigue hits hard, stops my pen mid-line; I don't want to account for all those descending leaves. *What are you going to do about it then?* asks toadflax. I muster a dog-leg scratched zigzag, wipe the nib off on the grass and go back inside.

10 October

My run takes me along the river to the mouth of the wood. I break a cobweb as I enter it. Scan ahead for plants: only brambles and withering bracken are still protruding through the litter of leaves.

Turning back, I pass tansy now scorched black. A line of silverweed engraves the grass.

I stop at a crop of white deadnettle (*Lamium album*), pinch off a flower and taste the sweet pale nectar at the tip. Roll it around in my mouth as I get out my notebook to draw. How might tasting a flower affect the drawing of it? It feels hairy on the tongue, much rougher than the pearly nubs seem to the eye. I peer in closer.

'If I had other senses, there are other things I should know,' observed Nan Shepherd, walking in the Cairngorm mountains a century ago. 'There must be many exciting properties of matter that we cannot know because we have no way to know them.'[65]

Can drawing function as another sense, one that combines looking with some empathic, hypothetical sense of touch? Today the practice of it feels something like extruded sight.

16 October

After days of rain, today is perfect drawing weather so I leave my desk early to pick the kids up. I'm going in search of a patch of white ivy-leaved toadflax I've spotted clinging to a wall on my route to the school. The white form is apparently quite rare – I was alerted to it by a laminated sign the council have put up on the nearby path: the same stretch of footpath they recently sprayed with herbicide. Thankfully, this wall seems to have been missed.

I find the toadflax, but my drawing comes out badly and I don't have time for a second attempt. When a drawing seems to fail it can be interesting to break down why, and this evening I look back at the drawing to assess what didn't work. It seems to show, for a start, some lack of fit between the marks I am making

10 October: white deadnettle (*Lamium album*)

11 October: shepherd's purse (*Capsella bursa-pastoris*)

with the pens I've got and the plant's own quality of outline. The toadflax leaves, each one composed of five Islamic arches, bear very few lines or traces on their surface, meaning that apart from silhouette there's very little I can mark to tether them to the page. Outline alone in such a decorative shape looks facile. There's a big change of scale from the largest leaves to the smallest: consequently, the youngest have ended up too chunky and the largest too finely or weakly drawn. It's a climbing plant, and the way it sprawls over the wall's capstone makes it cling to the page oddly; there's no sense of how it carries its weight in space. Perhaps I've also chosen too wide an area to deal with sufficiently.

These are some reasons I can identify for today's bad drawing; but perhaps there are plants that, even if I drew them a hundred times, would not fit my drawing body, my eyes' particular saccadic tendencies, my shoulder's or wrist's own manner of movement and mark. Perhaps there are plants with which I will never find the temporary kinship that falls through eye-brain-hand and onto a page. No algorithm could incorporate these ever-shifting variables and guarantee a winning formula. I love that fact, and find it paradoxically reassuring. The lack of any guarantees must be part of drawing's enduring fascination. You will always get a result you can't expect.

On my way back I pass the two ragworts that I drew a month ago, still holding up their flowers. I find myself nodding at them as at an old acquaintance.

18 October

The gardening column in the newspaper advises that if new weeds are still coming up it's a good sign you can still plant seeds for winter salads. Weeds are barometer and forecast.

18 October: Sunday morning

It's Sunday morning and the river is quiet. Only the runners are out, a few dog walkers and the older gentlemen who can't lie in. Little sound beyond the gulls on the water and the odd wing lapping at its surface. Half-buried in the sycamore leaf litter, new valerians are pushing up through gaps between the capstones. Fresh cleavers, juvenile green, bear softer rounded stars.

A tiny ivy is enamelling the fence post, its lines of leaves exquisitely arranged, alternately pointing right and left, right and left, away from the waxy stalk.

The grasses are carving slanted rectangles of cooling air.

Heron on the water: a punctuation mark.

Mounds of mallow are coming up in the heel of the wall. A maroon star marks the base of every leaf.

Metallic tang of damp nettle.

For the first time in months there's no yellow on this stretch of the river path. The plants are falling and subsiding in blackening heaps. The ragworts near the water's edge have given up earlier than the rest, succumbing to the damp.

By the gate is a sign I love. A white rectangle strapped to a metal post. Whatever was meant to be announced has been bleached clean away. Now it resolutely says nothing, just stops you and reflects the light, keeping silence.

20 October

My children find burdock seedheads (*Arctium* spp.) stuck to the dog's coat, pull them off and, feeling their stickiness, seek out more, hurling them at each other's backs. I fall back to watch another two humans discovering a game that must have been played for hundreds, maybe thousands of years. The throw, dodge and find again draws them ten minutes further along the path without complaint. Later I read that burdock inspired the invention of Velcro, after Swiss engineer George de Mestral found himself curious about how the burrs attached themselves so firmly to his own dog's coat, and discovered, looking at the barbed seeds under a microscope, hundreds of tiny hooks.

Back at the car I pull a dozen burrs off the children's shoulders and throw them out the window, marvelling at the sequence of movements the burdock has engineered in us. It's almost as if the plant's evolution has adopted 'play' as its means of dispersal.

Since we tend to regard plants as resources, available to serve our needs, it's easily forgotten that humans are also in the service of the plants that surround us. Plants have recruited all kinds of animals to be pollinators – most obviously insects, who are enticed and rewarded with sweet nectar. But the most effective *vectors* for plants are ourselves – our bodies, our transportation, our farming practices. 'Are we sure they haven't used their manipulative skills with us too, creating flowers, fruits, fragrances, and colours that please our species?' Stefano Mancuso asks in his fascinating study of plant intelligence, *Brilliant Green*. 'Without a doubt, it's humans who guarantee the reproduction, survival, and propagation of certain plant species to the detriment of others.'[66] One weed genus which has such a close relationship with human passage it might almost seem like a vegetal familiar is the greater or ribwort plantain.* In Britain, *Plantago major* and *Plantago lanceolata* are such a ubiquitous feature of footpaths, fields and grass that they often don't register as distinct plants. It

---

* That is, the *Plantago* family of flowering plants, not the banana-like fruits, which belong to a completely different genus (*Musa*).

helps that their rosettes of leaves lie tight to the ground, evading the mower, and usually matching the tones of the grass exactly. Plantains might be the weed exemplars of Richard Dawkins' phrase 'the anaesthetic of familiarity', so often seen merely as part of the texture of the ground. There are three of them in the foreground of Dürer's *Great Piece of Turf*.

Yet plantains were noted newcomers for indigenous Americans when the plant arrived there along with English settlers. In the seventeenth century, greater plantain spread so quickly and surely across the continent that it was named *English man's foot*, 'as though produced by their treading'.[67] The plant's uncommon resilience means it seems actively to benefit from trampling, although this may be because its competitors are more susceptible to being crushed. Plantains had already spread through Europe on the feet of Roman armies; more recently their seed was a contaminant of cereal grain and other crops, furthering its international dispersal. Along with docks and silverweed, plantains can be seen as part of 'the global signatures of disturbances', in Richard Mabey's eloquent phrase.[68]

Until the early twentieth century, merchant ships were often ballasted with quantities of earth. This earth would naturally contain all kinds of vegetal matter, including seed. The volume of the ballast would be adjusted, according to the changing cargo, to maintain the boat's consistent level in the water, involving transfers of soil collected and deposited at trading ports wherever the ship docked.

Along with humans and their herds of animals, ballast deposits became significant contributors to plant migration. In the late 1990s, botanist Heli Jutila discovered that the non-native flora on a nearby Finnish island were the result of plant stowaways in these deposits; more recently there has been increasing interest in the movement of plants as a document of human migration and colonial history.*

Given its historical links with the transatlantic slave trade, the city of Bristol makes a particularly emotive site for such research.** In 2012, Bristol's Arnolfini gallery commissioned an artwork by Brazilian artist Maria Thereza Alves which highlighted the capacity of plants to reanimate such histories quite literally, via an excavation of local ballast plants. Alvez collected earth from several sites around the historical trading port and, working with Heli Jutila and the University of Bristol Botanic Garden, used their expertise to select and germinate seeds from the extracted soil which had lain dormant for decades, even centuries. Local community groups, some of which had their own, personal links with other international ports, took part in growing the seedlings. The resulting plants were used to create a garden, planted in an appropriately transitory site on a barge in Bristol harbour.

---

* Three recent examples: in Northern Ireland, the exhibition *Fugitive Seeds* (2022), curated by Borbála Soós at CCA Londonderry, 'considers how endemic, alien and fugitive seeds connect to colonial histories including in Northern Ireland and more specifically Derry~Londonderry and its port' (www.ccadld.org/exhibitions/fugitive-seeds). In southern England, Bridget Anderson, Professor of Migration, Mobilities and Citizenship, and Jane Memmott, Professor of Ecology, both at Bristol University, collaborate on the guided walk 'What Can Weeds Tell Us About Migration?' as part of the Festival of Ideas, Bristol, 27 April 2023. In London, research at the Wellcome Trust into the impact of colonialism on indigenous plant knowledge was included in its 2022 exhibition *Rooted Beings*.

** 'In 1750 alone, Bristol ships transported some 8,000 of the 20,000 enslaved Africans sent that year to the British Caribbean and North America.' (www.bristolmuseums.org.uk/stories/bristol-transatlantic-slave-trade visited 30 March 2023)

Maria Thereza Alves, *Seeds of Change: A Floating Ballast Seed Garden* (Bristol), 2012–2016. Photo © Max McClure. Courtesy of Bristol City Council, Arnolfini and University of Bristol Botanic Garden

31 October: broom (*Cytisus scoparius*)

In Alves's work, *Seeds of Change: A Floating Ballast Seed Garden*, a garden becomes a document, a testimony. 'I've come to see these seeds as witnesses to complicated stories between us as people,' the artist has said.[69] But the plants grown from the seeds offer more than a document; they create a physical, public space – somewhere to visit and spend time in, and which, perhaps more than a gallery or library, offers material interaction with no requirement for a verbally articulated response. A garden is a place to be, no captioning necessary. Encountered through multiple senses including touch and scent, the flowering in Alves's garden becomes a kind of remembering, its diverse and complex geography recognising our own.

31 October

High winds. We head out of town, abandon the car in a lay-by and make for the shelter of the pine woods. Scent of horse manure and occasional coconut-whiff of gorse. The path to the wood is lined with a darkly exuberant tangle of bramble, gorse and broom, the latter's black seedpods shaking in faint, malevolent whispers. It's muddy after a week of rain, and tiny yellow hawthorn leaves imprint the purple earth; I'm glad of the low-lying brambles for providing grip. Hogweed is blown to 45 degrees and wind flutes through its hollow stems.

Across the hillside in front of me, flowering grasses lend a sandy glaze, almost iridescent with movement. The brambles have blackened and the willowherb is a mad scrawl across the hedge. In its midst, a single harebell – tiny miracle.

My children are playing a new game of wind-bathing – arms outstretched, backs to the wind, how many seconds can it hold you up before you fall. The gusts are thrilling but intense. I can't hear a thought in my head. Entering the forest feels like a reprieve.

I crouch by a pile of logs to draw. Next year's foxgloves are pushing up velvety leaves to begin. Strips of torn-off pine bark stripe the ground with their layered camo-pattern. All around me masses of something green are sprouting through the needles.

The cold brings precarity to my already shaky line. Imperceptible bits of things scud across the paper every few minutes and my hat is blown repeatedly over my eyes. I draw not knowing yet what this tiny weed is called, not recognising it – the twining, hair's-breadth stalks recall vetch, but without *Vicia*'s neat rows of leaves. Fumitory seems the closest, but this has tiny whitish flowers that look like damp tissue paper, not open yet, and giving the impression they might not bother doing so this late in the year.

Back at my desk and relieved to be out of the wind, the search for the weed's identity turns out to be as scrambling and tendrilled as the plant itself. Eventually an entry on Wikipedia, whose opening paragraph disparages 'a weak scrambling plant', tells me that Carl Linnaeus wrote of it as *Fumaria claviculata* or white climbing fumitory, *claviculata* referring to its tendrils. Somewhere along the line it was re-assigned Corydalis and is now known as *Ceratocapnos claviculata* – the climbing corydalis. I'm completely lost trying to follow the reasons for this evolving taxonomy, but impressed by the ability of this small, weak plant to repeatedly climb its way out of classification.

NOVEMBER

> Black star of cow parsley is fate
> in cellulose
>
> Sean Borodale, *Bee Journal*, 28 November[70]

A day as cold as it is still, the stillness a refusal of change. At the bend of the river is a stand of mugwort (*Artemisia vulgaris*), tall as a woman, perennially here. The fine-cut leaves, now darkening to pewter, turn macabre arabesques to show their silver undersides, glinting in the gloaming. Night's falling fast, nearer to wolf than dog, so I do what I've so far managed to avoid – break off a stem and take it home to draw under the light of my desk. There, holding the sodden-dark stalk in my left hand I drop my pen onto the page and begin wherever it lands. Too much to include it all – just follow a few inches to the paper's edge.

Of all the wild plants I've drawn, mugwort seems to me the witchiest: uncannily persistent through the winter, like a swaying body, its flowers clenched (technically daisies, but so small and tight as to preclude any sense of jollity), its foliage revealing a metallic face. No surprise to read of its history as

2 November: mugwort (*Artemisia vulgaris*)

a protective charm, hung over cottage doorways and carved around the heads of green men in medieval churches to ward off evil.* Its protective function extended to the everyday, too: the aromatic leaves used as treatment for nausea and worms, or as insect repellent (*mug* being an archaic word for *midge*). Looking at the sharply divided foliage, each leaflet twisting as it dries into some skewed baroque gesture, I wonder how many of the plant's ascribed properties were prompted by its ornamental form. Mugwort's ready-made curlicues are a gift to the craftsman, just itching to be drawn or cut with chisel. No other weed dies so exquisitely, twitching into silver.

I think back to a mugwort in the *Vienna Dioscorides*, its foliage drawn in unrealistic overabundance, as if the artist didn't want to finish. What hypnotic quality made him so reluctant to let this plant go?

4 November
Mallow stalks (*Malva sylvestris*): the green runs out halfway, leaving bleached and flowerless tips.

Tansy leaves hang from their stems in a sodden mass, shredded like some ancient garment.

Along the riverbank and through the paths that lead around the town, few weeds are continuing to flower – though some stalwarts will persist discreetly through the year, among them shepherd's purse, thale cress and chickweed. But those that are 'over' do not simply vanish. There's a huge amount still here, still bringing value both to ecosystem and observing eye. And,

---

* Notably, mugwort carvings decorate the early fourteenth–century roof bosses in Exeter Cathedral.

if Mancuso is right that the eye is part of that same ecosystem, these dying structures still beckon us to them. Many weeds, notably the umbellifers like cow parsley and hogweed, keep their seedheads through much of the winter, feeding birds and giving uplift and shape to the verges. Other, softer plants collapse and reduce to matted stuff which provides shelter for hibernating animals if we refrain from tidying it away too soon. And all of it, of course, will eventually rot down into the earth, aided and abetted by insects, fungi and microorganisms, to feed the soil for next year's growth.

There's something especially appealing about drawing plants that are 'going over'. It's partly the variety of states: the feverfew in my back garden is still producing new buds, tight new leaves and flowerheads with all their petals intact, but another lot of its stems are stiffening to brown, contorting into shapes of quiet anguish. The plant as a whole seems to have tired, giving in to a complication of leans or elbowings outward to accommodate its decline. A sense of struggle persists. It must be that it suits the way I draw, or want to approach a drawing – less fluid summary, more broken lines, acknowledging the plant's own effort and complexity with my own.

8 November

No time to draw, but a quick run down the river path with the dog, storing up things to come back to later.

Pellitory-of-the-wall is scrambling over the stonework, turning limestone the colour of faded green office files.

A yarrow head is tarnished copper. Its dessicated jerks in barely noticeable breeze show how light it has become since I was last here. (How long before it succumbs to damp and gravity?)

4 November: mallow (*Malva sylvestris*)

12 November: teasel (*Dipsacus fullonum*)

By the bench a single flowering stalk of rapeseed I first saw weeks ago, whose seed has drifted miles to get here, still flickers gently fluorescent on the path.

A wild dog rose has chosen a bad spot by the water's edge, grown upwards as far as it can, arching over now, finding nothing to cling to.

Still a froth of new growth though. Cleavers' innocent stars.

9 November
List of plants to check:

> black medick or hop trefoil?
> cuckoo flower or dame's rocket?
> black horehound or purple deadnettle?

I still have a long way to go in learning even the weeds I'm passing every day.

11 November
Brambles clothing the bank, their overlapping stitches like a giant darn, giving the ivied slope the lumpen contours of a human body.

12 November
First serious frost. I drop the kids at school and drive to the almost-edge of town where the main road north borders a wood. By the lay-by the field entrance is strewn with defunct fireworks, their cardboard cylinders now more soggy than declamatory. Frozen droplets hang glassily from the bars of the gate. Clover and vetch have stiffened in elegant attitudes.

A dark mass of teasel I haven't seen before pulls my eye over the fence.

I turn through the gate and stop dead. All the way down to the wood, the hogweed bordering the path is draped in luminous, backlit loops: spiders' webs, arcing from umbel to umbel as far as I can see.

On every visit, now, the wood is thinning. A kicking-thick rustle of leaves to walk through is poor compensation for the loss of its shielding canopy. Today, for the first time this autumn, I'm more aware of the breathy roar of the motorway than my own exhale. I stop to talk to a passing walker and find my chin has gone numb, blurring speech. Further into the wood I look for the tree I crouched beside to draw a forget-me-not last April. That place between its roots is inches deep in sycamore litter now: papery, black-spotted leaves which will break down and, with luck, further next year's flower. I mark a lichen on the trunk above with my thumbnail; a graffiti note-to-self.

Returning to the car, I draw a teasel (*Dipsacus fullonum*) standing near the path. No one about, but my head keeps turning, sensing an approach – only water, dropping as it thaws.

13 November

This is the time when I want to draw nettles, when the foliage has shrunk away leaving little but a taut and blackening stalk.

At the corner of the river path, a man is flying a drone. My dog sees it first, this scentless bird rising vertically as no living creature could. Eyes blink green and red as it curves off over the viaduct, away from the estuary. As I draw near, the man shows me what it sees, its picture filling the oblong of his screen. I see the whole arc of river path from 80 metres up. Is this really the place I have come to know in such familiar detail? A greyish curl of water bordered by more grey, edged raggedly with dull green fringe. A bank of cloud covers the sunrise he was hoping for. It looks like nothing.

14 November

The busiest streets now show few weeds. Though dirt still catches in the cracks in the paving, the plants that lodge there rarely manage to raise themselves above the surface of the slabs, the footfall and street-sweeping both too frequent for survival.

But you don't need to look far. Just off the high street, a wall pockmarked with loose render sprouts delicate ferns of maidenhair spleenwort from its crumbling seams. Pellitory-of-the-wall and ivy-leaved toadflax keep each other's hyphenated company. In the yard at the back of the shops, the rows of bins are stashed alongside sheets of chipboard and bowls of water for the local dogs; the pellitory makes a map of concrete cracks and toadflax inches forth across the tarmac. Moss covers up an unused corner of the pavement, apparently unbothered by the tracks of wheelie bins.

In the corner of a parking space, where dirt blows in and accumulates somehow into soil or else a medium that will do for now, valerian clumps beside a tuft of grass like the one dug up by Dürer. A now-superfluous stump of wall has grown a starry colony of purple toadflax. Beyond, the hotel's padlocked yard accrues low mounds of buddleia and filaments of hoary willowherb that flicker among the rusting cans. One drainpipe holds a shroud of greying cleavers. At its base a stonecrop; plastic shards of ultramarine, the fractured bottle tops of full cream milk, stand in for flowers.

Turning back onto the main street, the lack of green feels almost sinister, a kind of censorship.

15 November
No light has broken through all day but the dog needs walking and so do I, so we drag ourselves out to walk along the town's perimeter. Wet brings damp brings weight, and pallid light reflecting off the waxy surfaces of leaves. Scent, too. Not floral now but something older, earthier, more subterranean.

If I hadn't been following these plants over the preceding months it would be hard to see what's going on, or to care. 'It is not only what you actually see along the path,' observed the nineteenth-century nature writer Richard Jefferies, 'but what you remember to have seen, that gives it its beauty.' Is Jefferies talking about the necessity of palimpsest to provide depth and meaning? That it is what you remember having seen, *refracted through* what you are seeing now, that makes things compelling? A lot of grass has grown up since I was last here, yellowing and smothering the smaller plants. As flowers have withered and dropped, the clearest markers of identity have gone. And stems recognised by their upright shapes now fall over each other in a tangled mass, weighed down by wet leaf litter.

The unruliness of it brings relief – there's an energy to be drawn from the giving up. A sense of a return, a bedding-down or coming back to earth.

As we creep further into winter and the great reducing gathers pace, I'm thinking back to January, drawing that small tuft of grass when very few plants were raising their heads above the bone-cold streets. And of Perec's question, what happens when nothing happens? What will become more present as so much that has claimed attention falls away?

15 November: ragwort (*Jacobaea vulgaris*)

Perec's *Species of Spaces and Other Pieces* was published in Paris in 1974. The same year, in Mexico, artist Ana Mendieta was beginning to make a series of works that involved, in a very different way, an intimate questioning of her body and its relationship with place. As Perec submerged himself in a tissue of description, an exhaustive cataloguing of the metropolitan life around him, Mendieta buried her own body in the ground. Her three-minute silent film *Grass Breathing* shows a patch of grassy ground pockmarked with weeds; a central section of the turf is slightly raised, and lightly falls and rises with her breath.

Much of Mendieta's work resonates with unseen suffering, but the strange thing about *Grass Breathing* is that it doesn't seem expressive of a suffering body, despite the nightmarish scenario that might be imagined. The breathing remains measured, undisturbed; the body is combining with the ground with deliberate and uncanny calm.

The work is easier to understand in the context of Mendieta's exile from her home in Cuba at a young age. She spoke of her desire for 'a return to the maternal source' and much of her work embodies this sense of emplacement. 'I have no motherland, I feel a need to join with the earth,' she later asserted.[71] When she repeatedly inscribes the outline of her body onto the ground (*Siluetas* series, from 1978) there's the same underlying sense of longing, the same desire to erode the boundaries between self and landscape. Mendieta cuts or marks her outlines across the soil but, like Richard Long's, her works leave slight and organically reparable traces. And they are very simply and directly made: *Grass Breathing* runs the length of a roll of Super 8 film, no edits. As such, its looping lapse becomes an archetype of breathing, held out of time, rather than a documented performance.

As Dima Tolkachov experienced, witnessing the weeds that grew through shrapnel damage, the growth of common grass and weeds was also for Mendieta an evocation of time passing, a visual signifier of something unseeable, unfathomable.* And naturally, the grave-like form of *Grass Breathing* can't help but evoke the brevity of life. 'The days of man are but as grass,' as the psalm goes, 'for he flourisheth as a flower of the field / As soon as the wind goeth over it, it is gone.'[72]

Much of the imagery Mendieta created through her brutally abbreviated life employed the archetypical: it is lucid, symbolic, concise. *Grass Breathing*, though, is murky and unclear. A video still shows almost nothing. The speckled grass that fills the frame could read as photographic grain, the soft desaturated grain of Super 8. Mendieta chooses an unremarkable, quotidian patch of ground so indistinct it merges with the material of film itself, so that the work succeeds, where human limitations fail, in eliding body, landscape and artistic medium. *What are these boundaries we hold to between body and place, between human and non-human?* it seems to ask. Might they be more porous, and yet more mysterious, than we imagine?

19 November

A weekend walk, and we've agreed to make a stop: my daughter wants to write in her new diary and the ground is wet, so she

---

* '[T]hat growth reminded me of time,' Mendieta said of the grasses and weeds she saw in Mexico in 1973. The interview is cited in Ara Osterweil, 'Bodily Rites: The Films of Ana Mendieta', *ARTFORUM*, accessed 30 April 2023, https://www.artforum.com/print/201509/bodily-rites-the-films-of-ana-mendieta-55531.

19 November: cow parsley, new shoot (*Anthriscus sylvestris*)

has levered herself into a small tree; her limbs dangle like half-broken branches, mid-prune.

I'm scanning the ground for nearby foliage so that I can draw in her vicinity. Cow parsley: new shoots are coming up everywhere, just a few inches out of the ground. I kneel on an old carrier bag to get in close.

When it's flowering in May, cow parsley is all about the mass effect, but in these beginning plants you really notice how ornate its individual leaves are: two or three times pinnate, each ferny frond an exercise in subdivision. Approximating their complexity with a malfunctioning pen I make hard work of this, dipping the nib in the remnants of my coffee to loosen the encrusted ink, but the plant itself is burdened by no such labour or tension. Each leaflet is perfectly composed and overlaps its neighbours without distortion, the underneath frond curving gently down to give it space. A sense of effortless composure.

My daughter in her tree decides to try to take a nap; she can't achieve the necessary comfort, but I admire the wish, an instinctive move toward adapting to the plant via sleep's loosening of our outlines. This empathetic intermingling with the vegetal world, experienced so naturally by children, reminds me of the photographs of Simryn Gill, a Singapore-born, Australia-based artist whose work often involves an intimate handling of plants. It sometimes seems, in fact, as if she's making the work in order to facilitate that intimacy. In *Travelling Light* (2017) Gill draws the shoots of a coconut tree by inking them up and pressing them through her paper, slowly turning and clasping the plant to capture its surfaces as carefully as she can. This is drawing by feel, a way of working that bypasses vision – the artist can't see the image accruing on the reverse – and relies on the other senses

Simryn Gill, *Vegetation 3*, 1999
gelatin silver print, 27 x 27cm
© Simryn Gill, courtesy the artist

as a guide to the emerging inked impression. 'I just wanted to touch them,' Gill explained, 'that's what this way of drawing does [...] You feel every crevice and crack and in a way you see so much more clearly when your fingers are involved that you can't see with your eyes.'[73] It's that embodied cognition, again.

In her earlier series, *Vegetation* (1999), Gill used wild plants and shrubs to fashion disguises for her body, allowing her to begin to disappear into the landscape. (I remember my daughter, much younger, holding small branches of fir against her body, in the hope that, so concealed, she'd see a deer emerge from the depths of the wood.) 'I've always played with closeness,' as Gill put it, 'getting so close into things that you become them, you become part of a plant or part of a tree. If you want to make that as disguise for yourself or a covering, you have to really figure out how things come together.' As before, there is the sense of artistic process developed in the service of connection, rather than the reverse. The images in *Vegetation* play a game with authorship too, and plant-human hierarchies, as Gill stands in the centre of a dusty track, her head and shoulders covered in a thickety mass, occluding her identity. 'I disappeared myself, so who is working with who?'[74]

I love one particular image, *Vegetation 3*, not just for what Gill says about playing with closeness and using all of your body to get to know a plant. I love it for the way it works below language and logic. The figure standing shrouded in the plant is everything at once – funny and absurd, painful and beautiful, nonsensical and deep in thought. It's a representation both literal and surreal of the sympathies between plant structures and our own neurology, sympathies Oliver Sacks's observations hinted at. And after all, who doesn't recognise the experience of mind as an impenetrable

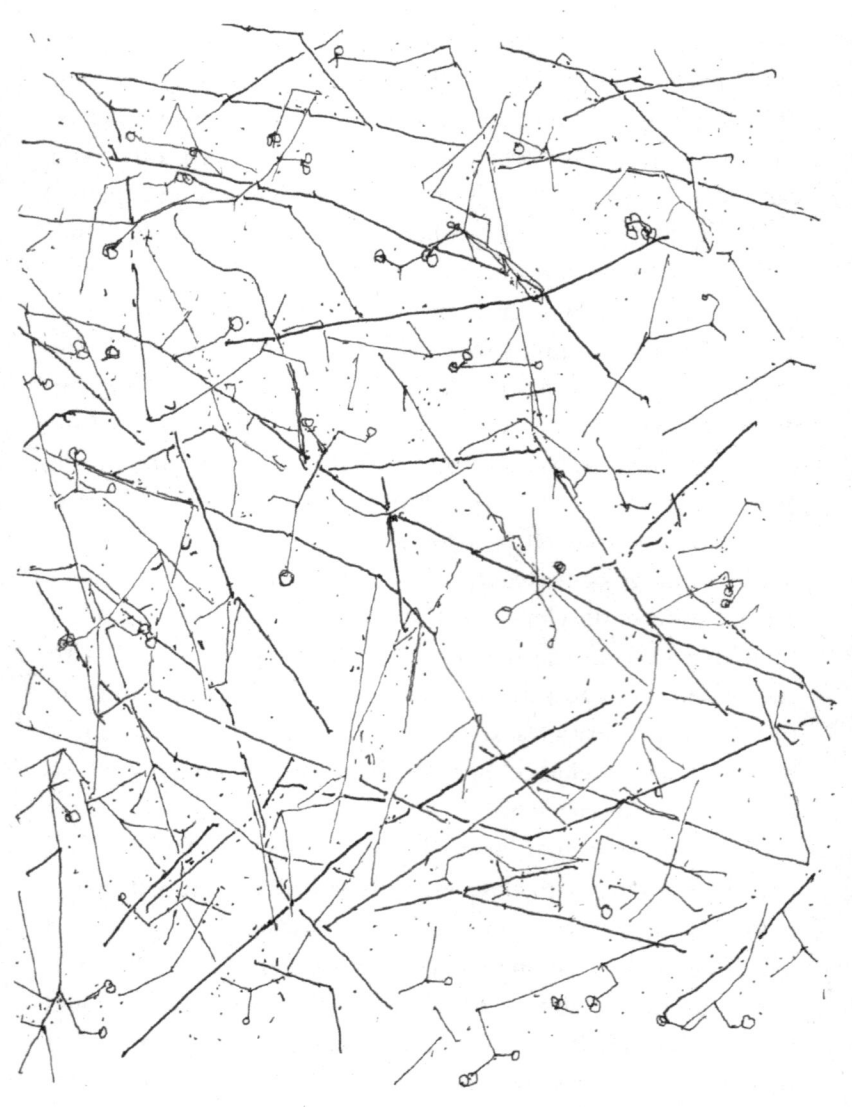

27 November: cleavers (*Galium aparine*)

thicket? Gill offers, then, an image of profound biophilia; and of what it might be like to put our exhausting human thinking aside for a minute, and stand as still and silent as a plant.

20 November
On the station path, splattered red hawthorn berries stamped into the pavement, juicier than they look intact. Ivy is in full flower. New growth on it too, the young leaves lime-green and soft to the touch, more rounded than their mature shape. Mallow skeletons now silver. Matted remnants of cleavers have fallen over the ivy bed like a layer of lace. The nettles are marbled with black – frost drawing its own damage. Traffic louder, with no leaf canopy to muffle the sound.

21 November
When I draw the seedheads of the nipplewort on the wall there is the memory of it in flower, but this form imprints more firmly on the backs of my eyes, perhaps because of the conjoined sound of the weed ringing itself as it trembles.

22 November
In the wood the bracken is drying in pained shapes beneath a litter of beech leaves; seedheads of wood avens branch madly, ending in velvety nubs. I draw soft-shield fern and grasses, looking at the shapes of spaces in between them. The more lines I add, the more lines I see; many of them probably aren't there.

27 November
At the edge of town, grim hanging flowers of the sedge, sour tang of remaining hogweed; the fretwork of cleavers gone

to seed falling over the bramble arches. Hawthorn berries darkening; Dürer's emerald picking out the light.

28 November

A constant presence across town, scrambling out of pavement cracks, climbing across walls and around lamp-posts, lodging in the seams of masonry anywhere it can, is pellitory-of-the-wall (*Parietaria judaica*). This is a weed possessing that combination of ubiquity and discretion that makes things dismissible, if not invisible. I've even missed its flowering – and admittedly I'm only properly turning to it now that so much else is falling away. Its flowers (I read, since they are over now) are tiny dots of greenish white, too small for me to make out their form even when I look them up in books; and, though there's more colour in the stems, their pinkish-brown tends, in my town at least, to merge with the sandstone backdrop.

It takes me three attempts to draw this weed, as if my sense of it as nondescript had literally stopped me from describing it in ink. Questioning that adjective, I check its etymology: *non-descriptus* (Latin), 1680s, from the past participle of *describere* (to write down, copy; sketch, represent) meaning 'not previously described'. It seems telling of the nature of attention that things dubbed indescribable we pay a lot of attention to describing, whilst those we struggle to take interest in are put aside and classed as 'not-yet dealt with'. Dull or undistinctive is almost etymologically linked to procrastination. Well, that feels true. In the case of pellitory, its green is at the buff end of the spectrum, made more drab by a lack of gloss, and the flowers are clearly small enough to go unnoticed. I also realise that its leaf shape is not registering in my visual memory even after I've drawn it.

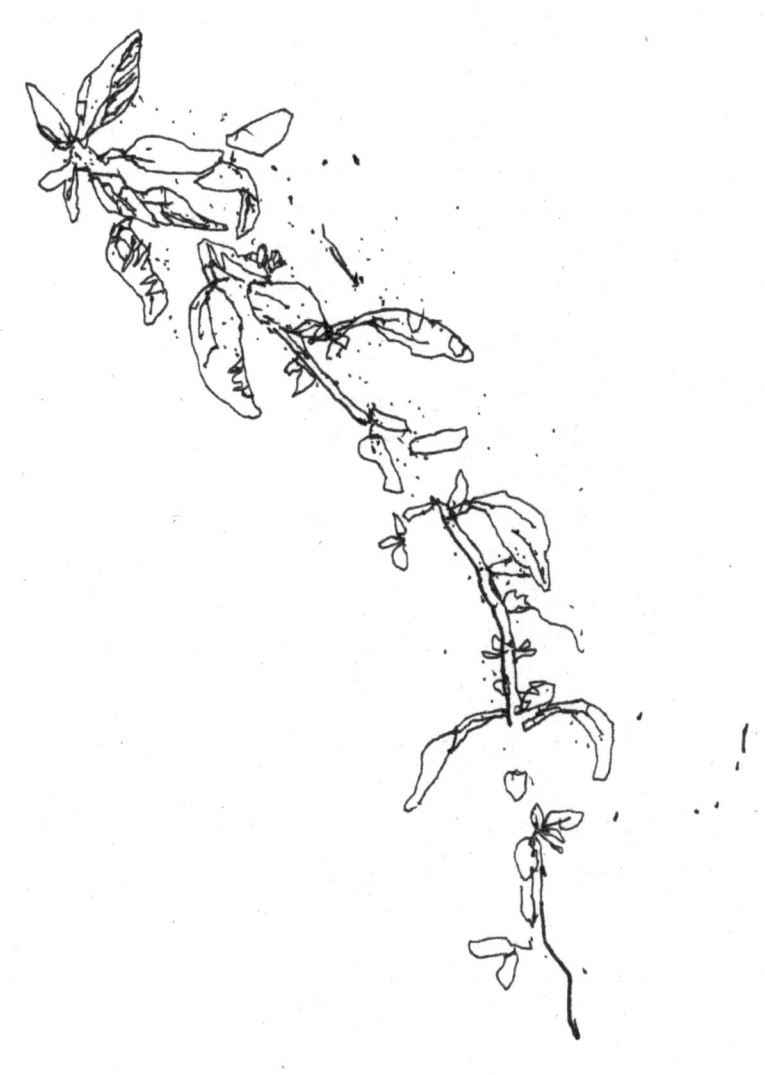

28 November: pellitory-of-the-wall (*Parietaria judaica*)

Pellitory's name derives from old French and Latin words for wall, so the name is an odd tautology – wall-of-the-wall.*

Despite the temporary frustration, the fact of making three drawings before I get one I'm at all satisfied with is oddly affirming. However many years I spend drawing, I know there will always be a certain elusive magic to it. With experience you learn things that help, and your intentions may get closer to their execution, but whatever it is you're trying to grasp will never quite be caught.

30 November

At the back of the high street shops, where bins are emptied, trolleys packed with broken-down cardboard and the lorries unload their deliveries, odd angles of yard that won't tessellate into use fill up with rusty stems of curly dock. A plot never quite confirmed for redevelopment has been colonised by willowherb, plants taking the initiative when no investor would. A nearby ramp, bollarded to prevent access, furs over with moss. Behind the library carpark and down a cut-through slope, tumbles of weeds and receipts collect together as if in sympathy with each other's unwantedness. Fallen pylons of shepherd's purse, bark scraps, pennycress, and corrugations of leaf and litter lift quietly from the tarmac. In a narrow alley that leads back to the high street, small strands of toadflax creep, relishing the damp.

I've made drawings in these places, and in more public streets, but I've drawn much more in the verdant spaces, around the edges of council parks, quiet side streets and down on the river path. Though I've said that rallying attention protects against

---

* Since it grows on stone, sympathetic magic decreed it should be used as a treatment for kidney stones.

self-consciousness, that claim was probably naive. Drawing is a kind of waiting, and shares its vulnerability, which has only sharpened since the sight of a waiting figure – a face without a phone screen to gaze into, forced to look out at the street – has virtually fallen out of existence.

For the drawer, sketching something recognised as worthwhile to record – a beautiful view, a picturesque corner of a city – will reassure the passerby; stand and draw an apparently empty patch of ground, though, and your presence is unsettling. If nothing is happening, perhaps something is about to.

DECEMBER

> I fingered the winter killed grass, looping it round the tip of my finger like hair, ruffling its tips with my palms. Another year has twined away, unrolled and dropped across nowhere like a flung banner painted in gibberish
>
> Annie Dillard, *Pilgrim at Tinker Creek*[75]

The first drawing, according to the ancient Greeks, was a drawing of a lover's shadow. Anticipating the departure of the man she loved, a young woman of Corinth turned to the wall and traced the outline of his sleeping profile with a charred fragment from the fire.* The first drawing was driven by impending loss: as perhaps all drawings are, consciously or not, navigating by means of line that temporary connection with what we're looking at, what we are about to lose.

The mythic origin of drawing reveals its inherent failure; a failure to preserve the object that is loved (if only by the eye).

---

* The story is related in the *Natural History* of Roman historian Pliny the Elder, and is supposed to have taken place around 600 BCE.

Mimesis can only be a shadow of the thing itself. A use of line admits this poverty openly, since nothing looks *outlined* like a drawing. But a line, of course, is not only a servant of mimesis, even when that might be what's required of it. As Paul Klee observed, a line can be taken for a walk. It can take the hand, the eye, the mind to unknown places, and to places of unknowing.

I walk my children up to school this morning, and it's oddly quiet. I'm thinking back across the countless times I've walked them up this path, the palimpsest of journeys as scuffed and reluctantly recalled as their uphill tread, and start to compile a mental list of all those things along the way that have made us stop, or meander sideways, made us late. The usual sensory attractions: breaking ice at puddle edges, smearing mud from shoes on damp grass, kicking at piles of leaves, stroking passing dogs. The discovery of loose stones that work as chalk, and the marking out of lines for some half-thought-out game. The unavoidable attraction to strange litter, discarded lighters, or unusual building-site detritus that might fit in a pocket; also the poring over of a pigeon carcass, dead mice, poor fledgling birds, and the urgent evacuation, after rain, of snails into the safety of the verge.

But we are growing out of, or away from, these digressions. Our walks along this path are getting swifter, easier and more unanimous. Less jolted by those halting about-turns, the interruptions of impromptu play. Our pace has gained consistency, smoothed both by greater filtering of what we encounter and a sense of resignation to the task. There's just less seizing upon it all. I suddenly see my children's childhood from above: the gradual straightening of a line, from here to there.

2 December: grasses

Is drawing substituting for the play I have lost? Play in its most basic sense of finding a way to be here, to negotiate or inhabit a place? What can happen when nothing is happening, or when what's taking place is just too much repeated, too ground in its tracks, too inevitable to feel 'live'?

Perhaps it has helped to make many of these drawings in the background of my children's games not just out of the urgency that gave me, not knowing how long I'd get, but from some echo of the open-endedness of their game. The not-knowing that is at the heart of play, not knowing what litter you might find or what weeds will be coming up, is also the not-knowing required to mark down what you really see.

To see something is to forget its name. However many times I start a drawing, my thinking mind will tell me: I know what this is, how a stem goes and a leaf joins on, how the other side will be the same, what sort of shape this thing looks like. Four decades I've been drawing and I'm still fighting cognitive gravity every time. You have to keep remembering that you don't know. Each leaf edge, each seed tip, each section of a stalk is different from your store of preconceptions – even those you've only just conceived. If you want to draw this flower or leaf and not the one before, you need to keep forgetting its identity.

I think of this slippery combination of determination and indeterminacy as being close to John Keats's 'negative capability'; the poet's realisation, described to his brothers in winter 1817, that an essential quality of any creative attempt is this ability to sit with not-knowing: to allow that which is doubtful or mysterious to remain so. 'I mean *Negative Capability*,' he explained, 'that is when man is capable of being in uncertainties, Mysteries, doubts, without any irritable reaching after fact & reason.'[76] On a micro level, drawing can offer a process for sustaining such uncertainty, for keeping the window open. The questioning line that's practised on the outline of a leaf might continue, invisibly, as attention's thread.

The drawings I have made in this year of weeds are very simple: barely artworks, even if the larger project of a year's attention to them might be considered so. Yet with each one, the sense of not-knowing how to begin or how to deal with the information I'm looking at, persists, along with the more deliberate practice of maintaining uncertainty in what is seen. Donald Barthelme described a writer as 'one who, embarking upon a task, does not know what to do'.[77] The same might be said of those of us who draw, who must begin not just by forgetting the name of the thing and its attendant preconceived images, but by finding a sense of bafflement. Interviewed at the peak of his success, Alberto Giacometti observed, 'I try to do the same thing that I found impossible to do thirty years ago. It seems as impossible to me now as it was then, totally impossible even, all it can lead to is failure.'[78] Bafflement is the best way to begin. The best way to make sure the moment is new.

In this, the weeds might be ideal collaborators: our plant familiars, who will always resist prediction and control. The aleatoric characters in the unknown drama of the street.

4 December

The days are rapidly darkening, the streets too. Along the high street, another stagger of shops are closing down, some reopening in expanded form at the new out-of-town shopping centre. We drive up there this weekend and find ourselves patrolling mile-long aisles of bright confectionery in a daze; moving, along with half the town, like pixellated animations in some early video game where you can only proceed at right angles or straight ahead. The massive warehouse edifices have been partially timber-clad, presumably in an effort to reassure us that they are still buildings. But all the infrastructure, sealed naturally against nature's incursions, is still so new there's no failure in it yet, no particularity. Only as you drive back to the roundabout do you see the mounds of earth shored up from its construction, huge purplish heaps, studded all over with bright emerald weeds. Soon all of it will green over and sink into memory.

Watching a succession of such weeds colonise another huge construction site, Richard Mabey wrote of his attempt to understand the place of these plants in the turmoil of human construction and abandonment. 'It occurs to me that they are like a kind of immune system,' he concluded, 'organisms which move in to repair damaged tissue, in this case earth stripped of its previous vegetation.'[79] It is known that weeds improve the soil and local environment in a multitude of ways, not least by acting as a carbon sink. As ground cover they protect the soil from drying out, stabilising and lessening the effects of erosion by wind or water. Capturing light and water and then dying back, they return key nutrients to the soil. And those with long taproots in particular, such as comfrey, bring minerals up from depths beyond the reach of other plants, returning them to the nutrient cycle.

Humans have exploited these capabilities with mixed success. In permaculture and in restoration ecology, weeds are increasingly understood and valued as reparative mechanisms, stewards of the soil which gardeners or farmers recognise for their role in supporting the wider ecosystem – and potentially as a source of food themselves. But the pioneer-vigour of some weeds, a capacity which allows them to colonise inhospitable environments so quickly and effectively, can also make them devastating. An egregious example is the Japanese kudzu vine (*Pueraria* sp.).

On my computer screen, a figure walks through a dense green tract of kudzu, idly resting a hand on its surface, stopping here and there, letting the trailing strands pass through their fingers. Odd stems rise above the rest in the shape of question marks. Half buried in the vine are six other standing bodies: totem-like and taller than life-size, each torso a mass of raw black sheepswool bound tightly into shape. The kudzu reaches up around their skirts, encircling their waists.

This is *Earthseed* (2020) – an installation by Nigerian-American artist-poet Precious Okoyomon at the Museum für Moderne Kunst, Frankfurt. In the video I watch online, the gallery becomes topography for performance as Okoyomon moves among the plants, now reading aloud, now listening to others reading via video call. Okoyomon has used kudzu repeatedly in their installations – including burnt, as ash – in interactions with the vine that reach back to a plant cutting taken aged fifteen. Their use of a vigorous, rampantly climbing weed as material cedes artistic control to an unpredictable creative force; the plant becomes an active collaborator. Though a path is cut through, the form and extent of the installation are otherwise determined by the kudzu's growth. But the choice of this particular weed is not only botanical. This is a plant whose history is suffused with suffering.

Kudzu vine was introduced to America from Asia by the US government in 1876 in an attempt to repair soil in southern states that had been devastated by the overcultivation of cotton, on plantations built on the labour of enslaved people. Kudzu was

Precious Okoyomon, *Earthseed*, 2020
kudzu vine, raw black lambswool, dirt, wire; dimensions variable
Museum for Modern Art, Frankfurt
© Precious Okoyomon, courtesy Museum für Moderne Kunst,
Frankfurt. Photo: Axel Schneider, Frankfurt am Main

5 December: nettles (*Urtica dioica*)

chosen because, as a member of the pea family, it not only grows extremely fast but fixes nitrogen, improving soil fertility. But the initiative backfired when the vine proved capable of spreading up to 100 feet in its new habitat, outcompeting native plants so mercilessly that existing vegetation, shrubs and even trees were smothered. Kudzu earned the moniker 'the vine that ate the South'.

A disastrous response to the double exploitation of slave labour and landscape, kudzu is now found in thirty-two states, and remains a complex symbol of racial and environmental harm. 'Soil memory is important to me, especially how plants remember history,' Okoyomon has said. 'Kudzu grows in some of the most racist parts of America for a very specific reason. The soil did not forget.'[80] Cotton is still a notoriously challenging and environmentally damaging crop to grow: particularly susceptible to severe weather and attacks from pests, it is globally one of the most pesticide-intensive crops. Like the weeds that flourish across sites of military conflict, in Okoyomon's work a weed's enduring vigour becomes testament to a legacy of trauma and the need for reparation; its perennial return an analogue of memory and the impossibility of erasure.

5 December

Out early with the dog. The light is pale and low, and the bank of ivy in front of me is a glassy, pallid blue. How often we insist on seeing plants as green, foreknowledge clasping object to its hue, despite the understanding that all colour is only reflected light and therefore mutable. No colour can be said to be embedded in the material of things in the way that we perceive it to be. The ascription of colour is memory's fiction, telling only how an object looked in some remembered paradigm of circumstance.

In the grass at the edge of the carpark, a few green streaks persist but, rather than enlivening the dead bleached stalks, their colour throws the subtle calibration off scale. I look around, failing to register anything; it all looks utterly discountable, as if, absurdly, the plants are refusing to be seen.

Casting my mind back to Perec's instructions, I remember he is strict on this. 'You must set about it more slowly, almost stupidly. Force yourself to write down what is of no interest, what is most obvious, most common, most colourless [...] Don't say, don't write "etc.",' he admonishes. 'You still haven't looked at anything, you've merely picked out what you've long ago picked out.'[81] His words might be instructions for drawing.

I can't help noting, though, that Perec conducted his observing from a café terrace near the Boulevard Saint-Germain, beer in hand. Hardly the most challenging of circumstances. I head towards home and coffee.

6 December
A walk down from the station through dark clods of moss, fallen from the gutters of tile-slipped roofs. Everywhere I look I seem to find some shrivelling waste; frost blunting at the tips, stalks falling forward to break at bleak angles.

Grasses congregate in withered, flattened humps; honesty's moon panes are torn away, leaving empty wire frames. In the crumbling seams of masonry, sowthistles make their desultory beginnings; tall stems of nettles bear their shrunken, darkened edges.

I take the shortcut between a block of flats and a row of garages. The small carpark is fringed with sparse, dead weeds. Remnants of more nettles, shepherd's purse, the ever-present groundsel. I

6 December: sparse remnants

9 December: sowthistle (*Sonchus* spp.)

stop to wait a while for the plants to register, trying again after yesterday's aborted attempt, and this time the sight of it sinks in. When there is little left save for a tangle of weightless stalks, there is a kind of release – each plant freed from the experience of itself as particular and known. As it disintegrates, it shrugs off identity and attendant expectations, expands into a more whole idea or experience of a plant: an essential identity barely describable in words, just as its appearance can barely now be drawn.

8 December

On the hillside, my eye is caught by a sprig of bittercress or somesuch. I skid to a stop and tell the others to carry on, I'll catch them up. Drop down and begin to draw this small beginning of a plant. It'll be a modest drawing, a brief and undemanding task.

I work my way down the stem, calling off my attempt where the stalk pinkens and delves into the ground, the privacy of that oddly moving. I look up to see my children in the distance, the distance of my outstretched arm, nearing the bottom of the hill. Some sort of inchoate calculation hovers along with my nib; time and distance, a sprig of bittercress and the few minutes it's taken to record, the same few minutes it takes for three figures to reach the foot of the slope. My pen feels like the pivot point, one of an infinite number of such fulcra about which it all hovers. A small spider crosses the stem and re-enters the unknowable grass.

9 December

Another storm has rocked the night. Flung across the tarmac is a lichenous alphabet – tiny fragments of furred and rotting twigs. The stalks of sycamore leaves have been stripped of their foliage and lie strewn over the path in a slack, green cursive.

Against a wall a single sowthistle stands in flower, holding fast against the wind. Its stem is muscular, purplish. Lax clusters of buds atop the branching stalks resemble the onion-domes of Orthodox cathedrals, their dandelion-flowers now withered to stumps of burnt orange. The leaves, prickled only sparsely and without malice, are frostbitten now and terminate in crumbling tips, a comment trailing off to nothing.

The sowthistle's stalwart meagreness, its tremble and its wavering profile seem to match the movements of my half-numb hands, the tension in a body held stiff with cold. Best not to be too prepared, to draw in winter. Bring the wrong materials, insufficient ink, ungloved hands. Meet the plant on its own terms, dulled by the winter's effort at remaining.

10 December
On my way back from the shops, I find myself detouring to check in on the sowthistle again. Its leaves are drier now and the crisping at the edges is spreading inward. The leftward lean is more pronounced. A few more of the flowers have gone over. But there's something else, as well – some impression of a former intimacy. A sensation not only of the past flower, but of my past self here, two days ago. Through the drawn encounter, the plant allows me to recognise myself, passing.

12 December
Middle of the night. I'm lying in a hotel room in the dark, thinking back across the year. The image floats up of a tabulated calendar, sprouting weeds through all its seams: the slivers of time found in between work and family, between and through the public, social and domestic stuff of life. Will all this time

I've spent drawing plants help me get nearer to drawing my own face? Or even just to seeing my face, the actual expanse of tissue-covered bone beneath the palimpsest of opinions, projections, desires and dissatisfactions, the accretions of memories of looking and all the rest that clouds the mirror most of the time?

Night can help too, of course. The isolation of a nocturnal space helps separate them out: voices rising to the surface to be skimmed off. I get up and fumble for my notebook in the dark.

I know so much more about my face than I do about the plants, and I'm more invested in its contours; there's almost nothing less neutral I could draw. Yet still, the pattern of approach built up in front of weeds, the looping, continuous rhythms of looking out and then down at the paper, of putting aside what I think I know to ask *how does it appear, really?* – I'm reassured to find now supports me here, standing sleepless by a mirror, in a Premier Inn bathroom in the middle of the night.

I turn the tap to run a minute river through my nib, black rivulets of ink marking the ceramic, phone torch illuminating the glass so I don't alert the fan, and look up.

It turns out that this mouth, through which all day I utter myself, is hardly important at all. Just a brief horizontal through its centre where the lips meet (pulling down a little at each side into a patch of shadow, another small descent of age I'm supposed to regret). I mark the upper lip's edge before I can stop myself but there's no real line here, only a change in colour. On the other hand, the sides – *cheeks* seems too round a word – where what I think of as my face slides back into my ears and hair, seem both weirdly important and sad. I can't make out where the confines are, can't mark those sides of myself as edges; I'm at a loss. A face is not an oval at the front with sides a separate plane. It's more of a falling away. A lapsing of myself into a shadowy blur.

14 December

I'm heading east as the sun is coming up pink, its light reflecting off the wet road gleaming rose. Puddles are pools of it. I'm bathing in this extra light, so welcome after a dark passage of days. Along the path that skirts the motorway I see a white mark in the verge: bladder campion (*Silene vulgaris*), unseasonably in flower. The division of its petals is complicated by decay, and its leaves are rusted, speckled orange-brown. But it's here nonetheless, defying all the calendars of the wildflower guides.

At the opening of the wood, the path becomes so muddy that I'm forced to slow right down and carefully modulate my weight to keep my balance. I aim for the tree roots on either side for grip. New growth is coming through everywhere: brambles, wood avens, creeping buttercup; small ferns of cow parsley, a froth of cleavers. New dandelions emerging, and the first patch of celandine leaves, tiny hearts less than a centimetre across, whose flowers I can start to look for in the new year.

I turn to draw a small new shoot of wood avens, which will be tipped in yellow flowers by the spring. On the smallest of its leaves the lines of veins are deeply furrowed. It's clear that they are still in the act of fully opening, slowly smoothing and spreading to their proper shape. As I follow the creases with my pen, my mind arcs back to my newborn daughter a decade ago, and the delicate curled folds on the tops of her ears, a temporary creasing which took a few days to unfurl.

When I question what moves me about this, it's not the uncurling avens leaf or the memory of my newborn's ears

14 December: wood avens (*Geum urbanum*), new shoot

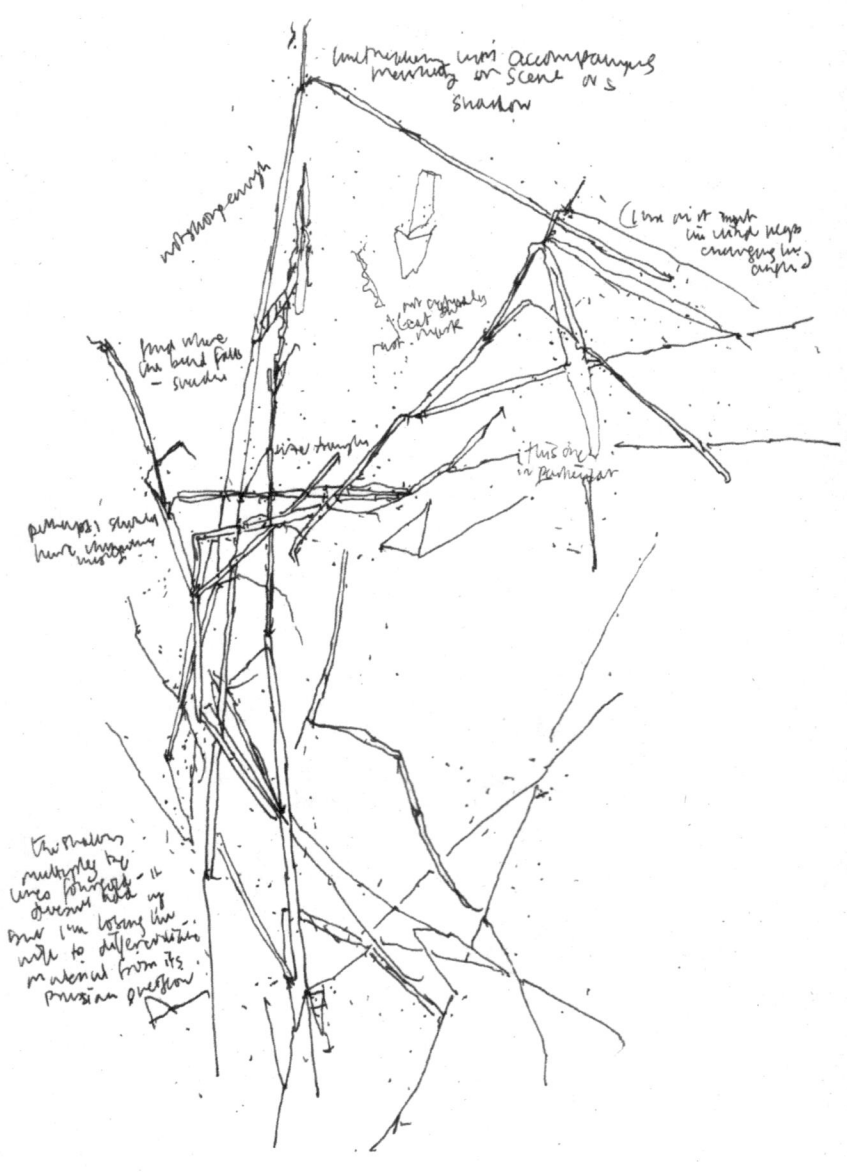

22 December: grasses in a ditch

– though both are beautiful to me – but the connection between them: a thread like some mycelial fibre underground, linking this new organism unfurling in the forest with another uncurling in a hospital room years ago.

Reading about wood avens later in the day, I find another common name for it, herb bennet, comes from the Latin for 'a blessed herb' (*herba benedicta*). In the medieval herbal *Ortus Sanitatis*, the plant was blessed above all others for the spicy, clove-like fragrance of its roots.

18 December

We are grinding to a halt before the year's turn.

In the marketplace, I watch a man singing, turned away from me to face the crowd. He is elderly, and the back of his neck is as furrowed and puckered as the surface of a dock leaf.

20 December

Ivy gives off so much light – and when you need it most.

22 December

I scan my mental image of the riverbank. What's left there now, still standing in the collapse of the year's end? I'm heading for the turn in the path where I know mugwort grows, but when I reach it the light is so low and bright that I can't look at it, and see no more than a silhouetted clump. I turn my back on the sun and my eyes fall gratefully on the verge. Grasses are pulling themselves up out of the ditch, carving acute triangles of air.

As I draw, the shadows seem to multiply the stalks fourfold; it doesn't add up. But as the inky lines accrue it seems to matter less and less what's vegetal and what's light, or lack of it. Now, with the setting sun behind me almost at the horizon, I absorb plant shadows into the common shade of my body. My weight shifts foot to foot, I feel my breadth affect the relative obscurity of the grass. How strange to understand a shadow as a lack, when it stains this deep a blue.

My thinking mind is leaking onto the paper now. Some odd phrase, sensation or scent memory, a line of a conversation from a TV show. A domestic memo jerks from the nib, the words emerging in the scrawled mark of the drawing. A complicated disarray of lines that echoes the confusion of the grass.

27 December
In the cracks in the street only ryegrass persists.

28 December
The holidays over, I take the train into the city to meet a friend. Above the door, the destinations scroll in ribbons of lime-green lights. Rough seat velour pricks at the backs of our heads. Our nails tap tenderly against the glass of our tiny screens. Shunting movements elongate odd bursts of laughter as the carriage rocks on its tracks. The flickering oblongs pull our faces downward, chins slumping resignedly into coats.

Here and there small, high-pitched sounds leak across the aisle: points scored on a game, the digital suck of a camera shutter, a distant half of a conversation, a TV chef making a salad. Private, unfathomable, disconnected, the content seeps from our devices like the utterings of disturbed folks in the street. Only these sounds are frictionless, all weight removed, and no one is watching. At intervals some new noise bursts out unexpectedly; a quick side glance or resetting of the shoulders betrays a flicker of shame, but it's swiftly pushed back by the next bright image. We sit mutely, faces illuminated by our screens, the carriage a safe zone in which to admit our inability to wait.

Nothing is harder to do than doing nothing. Boredom, the psychoanalytic writer Adam Phillips has observed, 'returns us to the scene of inquiry, to the poverty of our curiosity, and the simple question, What does one want to do with one's time?' We accept boredom as a necessary condition of childhood – or we did until recently – but for adults it becomes a state of real uncertainty that seems to threaten, even, to unravel us. 'After all, who can wait for nothing?'[82]

Drawing might be defined as a particular kind of waiting, which records its own interval via marks made on paper. To draw is to wait for these lines to accrue into something recognised as present; it may also be to wait for life to resume. I know that drawing can offer a temporary place to hide, which might be useful, especially, for the kind of mind that tends to watch for too much detail.

Back in my studio, I'm working on a new drawing: a large-scale image of a patch of grass in which some lines of words emerge as absences of vegetation. I'm using brush and ink – indigo, that shadow blue that stains the grass in early evening.

How do you register and record the experience of being here, the ongoingness in the static image? If a drawing contains the amount of time it took to make, can it offer solace, this shoring up of time tracked by an observing body?

Ultimately, drawing is only a mechanism to keep on looking, the drawn line a means of fastening your attention to what's there. And while a drawing marks a failure to preserve the

29 December: hogweed (*Heracleum sphondylium*)

thing itself, or even to recognise it adequately, it preserves that failure, that effort at connection, and helps you keep on trying to connect. *Fail again, fail better.* The unintended deviations of a line, like the ribs of an ox-eye daisy stem revealed by Blossfeldt's lens, the wandering arc of a bramble that invades a page of manuscript, or the weeds of any kind that disrupt the straight line of the street, are what make it enduringly compelling. It is the errantness of the line which proves it's *live*.

It's late now, the sky the indigo of my ink. My son comes into my studio unable to sleep, and I make him up a bed in the corner with an old sofa cushion. Lying on his side watching me, he slowly and sleepily picks out the words in my drawing. 'What happens when nothing happens?' he reads. 'Well, there is always sound,' he says, 'even if it's just your joints creaking.'

29 December

In the woods, I hang back to watch my son moving through the trees ahead. Those banks of umbellifers are giving up now: collapsing at jazzy, downbeat angles. We are at the hinge of the year and it is creaking on the turn. Dampness in the stalks of everything, they haven't got a hope; in the pages of my book, too, and the air as it comes in.

The sound is heavily compressed and it's often unclear whether that's breath, or the hiss of fine twigs snapping. His pace through the wood is the same: steadied by the thicket, but incorporating small changes in tempo; meandering, aimless, yet gently purposeful – aimless in that there's no deliberate intent, but propelled by open-ended curiosity …

Now he pushes his way through thickety stuff. Why, when there is a clear path?

Like when he runs a stick along a fence or sleeve along a wall. You can see it in the wearing and tearing of his clothes. A need for feedback.

Singing a wandering, made-up tune, dithery but consistent, no drama, small intervals between the notes, repeated fourths. Sound waves reverberate in the body, reflect off the stone, the trunks of trees, meet crackling sounds of dried wood-litter underfoot.

At my feet, tiny, muted movements as the stalks of trampled grasses try to right themselves, the almost unnoticeable after-effects of him passing, a minute ago.

POSTSCRIPT

I'm once again at the National Gallery, with time enough to see one favourite artwork. A pair of gilded panels hinged together like a book, painted six centuries ago in either England or France, a very rare survival: the Wilton Diptych. An outer panel shows a white stag lying in the grass, apparently on a bed of rosemary, ferns and speedwells. The tiny flower glimpsed at his feet, which might be a scarlet pimpernel, is the same weed I will draw in the shrubbery of an airport carpark, nine months from now.

Whoever painted the grassy bank above did so with the knowledge that no two blades of grass are ever the same. Each stem is distinct and each moves differently in its fourteenth-century breeze. It looks to me as though there were once other weeds in flower in the sward: small petal-sized areas of gold are missing, floating absences near the longer stems, revealing patches of burnt umber underneath. The grass looks blackened with time, but not so differently from the way it does in low evening sun, when seen in backlit silhouette. Wandering horizontal cracks disturb the surface like the lines of distant hills.

The close of this year is really the close of several years of drawing weeds, and at the same time it remains unfinished. I still walk out with notebook and pen, if more sporadically.

The Wilton Diptych, c.1395–1399 [detail]
egg tempera on oak, 53 x 37cm
National Gallery, London

POSTSCRIPT

'Knowledge does not dispel mystery,' as Nan Shepherd observed after decades studying her own surrounding landscape. 'The thing to be known grows with the knowing'.[83] I'm reassured that it could never be completed, this looking-tracking of the plants along the streets, since every weed will come up differently to the last, battered both by different weather and different memories of itself.

ACKNOWLEDGEMENTS

Sincere thanks to my agent, Seren Adams, for believing in this book and guiding it to the right eyes. And to all at Duckworth, particularly my editor Rowan Cope, who gave the book a home and shepherded it to publication with such insight and care.

Loving thanks to Kate, Vicky, Katerina, Kirstie, Aurora and Claire, who read pages at different stages and offered such thoughtful feedback and encouragement. To Georgie for invaluable advice and help. To the wonderful CommonRoom for the opportunity to make a sixth-century bramble into wallpaper. And to Jessie, Jules, Claire, Gillian and Sari for writerly support and friendship.

I am very grateful to Moniack Mhor, Scotland's Creative Writing Centre, for a bursary enabling a writing week in the Highlands which brought many enriching conversations around eco-poetics, both with my fellow residents, and with generous tutors Jen Hadfield and James Goodman. Thank you to Professor Alixe Bovey, for such an inspiring introduction to the Vienna Dioscorides, among several other manuscripts. Thanks also to The Artists Information Company and the North East Artists' Fund for supporting research time and travel.

Sincere thanks to the Society of Authors for a grant which enabled the completion of this book.

ACKNOWLEDGEMENTS

Heartfelt thanks to my mother Diana, and to all my wider family for support in myriad ways. To F & M for constantly returning me to the necessary bafflement, teaching me so much about attention, and prompting me to seize upon the gaps. And to Martin, for unfailing kindness.

NOTES

Before
1   John Berger, *Bento's Sketchbook* (London: Verso, 2015), 10.

January
2   Paul Virilio, 'On Georges Perec', AA Files, no.45/46 (London: Architectural Association School of Architecture, 2001), 15.
3   At the opening of *An Attempt at Exhausting a Place in Paris*, Perec explains his endeavour to describe 'that which is generally not taken note of, that which is not noticed, that which has no importance: what happens when nothing happens other than the weather, people, cars, and clouds.' Translated Marc Lowenthal (Cambridge, Massachusetts: Wakefield Press), 3. The question also pervades several of his other essays.
4   Annie Dillard, *Pilgrim at Tinker Creek* (Norwich: Canterbury Press, 2011), 200.
5   Richard Jefferies, *Nature Diaries* quoted in Geoffrey Grigson, *The English Year from Diaries and Letters* (Oxford: Oxford University Press, 1984), 6.

February
6   John McGahern, *That They May Face the Rising Sun* (London: Faber and Faber, 2002), 64.

March
7   Etel Adnan, 'The morning after / my death' in *The Spring Flowers Own & The Manifestations of the Voyage* (Sausalito: Post-Apollo Press, 1990).
8   *Urtica dioica* from O.W. Thomé, *Flora von Deutschland, Österreich und der Schweiz* (1885).
9   Molly Malone Cook and Mary Oliver, *Our World* (Boston, Mass.: Beacon Press, 2009), 71.
10   Ibid.

April
11   Richard Mabey, *Weeds: The Story of Outlaw Plants* (London: Profile Books, 2010).
12   Ibid.
13   Rosamond Richardson, *Britain's Wild Flowers: A Treasury of Traditions, Superstitions, Remedies and Literature* (London: National Trust, 2017), 247.
14   Nan Shepherd, *The Living Mountain: A Celebration of the Cairngorm Mountains of Scotland* (Edinburgh: Canongate, 2011), 41.

15 Philip Larkin, 'The Trees' (1974). in *The Complete Poems of Philip Larkin*, (London: Faber & Faber, London, 2014).
16 See 'Alternative Methods in Weed Management to the Use of Glyphosate', a report published by Pesticide Action Network Europe; (Brussels, 2023). Available to download at www.pan-uk.org
17 Monograph authored by a working group of seventeen experts from eleven countries, published in March 2015. https://www.iarc.who.int/featured-news/media-centre-iarc-news-glyphosate

May
18 John Cage, *Silence: Lectures and Writings* (Reprint edition, London: Marion Boyars, 2022), 96.
19 Derek Jarman and Howard Sooley, *Derek Jarman's Garden* (Reprint edition, London: Thames & Hudson, 2018), 53.
20 Joan Didion, *We Tell Ourselves Stories in Order to Live: Collected Nonfiction* (Everyman's Library edition, New York: Alfred A. Knopf, 2006).
21 Gerard Manley Hopkins, 'Spring' from Gerard Manley Hopkins, in *Poems and Prose* (Reprint edition, London: Penguin Classics, 2008).
22 British Library manuscript reference Egerton 747; c.1280–1310. A digital facsimile of the herbal can be viewed via the British Library website.
23 William Turner, quoted in Richardson, *Britain's Wild Flowers*.

June
24 Alice Oswald, *Weeds and Wild Flowers* (London: Faber and Faber, 2009).
25 Derek Walcott, *The Prodigal* (London: Faber and Faber, 2005).
26 *King James Bible*; Matthew 13:24–30.
27 Geoffrey Grigson, *The Englishman's Flora: Illustrated with Woodcuts from Sixteenth-Century Herbals* (London: Phoenix House, 1955), 305.
28 I was introduced to this work during a fascinating online research seminar given by Professor Alixe Bovey at the Courtauld Institute of Art, 19 June 2020.
29 Observed in Jules Jannick and Kim E. Hummer, 'The 1500th Anniversary (512–2012) of the Juliana Anicia Codex: An Illustrated Dioscoridean Recension', *Chronica Horticulturae* 52, no. 3 (2012).
30 John Clare, 'May' in *A Shepherd's Calendar* (1827).
31 John Clare to Eliza Emmerson, 1829, in *The Letters of John Clare*, edited by Mark Storey (Oxford: Oxford University Press, 1985), 491.
32 John Berger, *What Time Is It?* (Illustrated edition, Honiton: Notting Hill Editions, 2019).

July
33 Thomas A. Clark and Olwen Shone, *Distance and Proximity*, edited by Alec Finlay, (Edinburgh: Polygon, 2001).
34 In an interview with Gavin Esler for BBC's *Newsnight*, 2011).
35 On the artist's website at www.dorothycross.com/2019-2010/foxgloves
36 Sophy Roberts [@sophy_roberts], Instagram post, 23 August 2022 (retrieved 2 March 2023).
37 Laurence Scott, *The Four-Dimensional Human: Ways of Being in the Digital World* (London: Windmill Books, 2016), xv.

August

38　Dean Young, 'Selected Recent and New Errors', first published in *Poetry*, July–August 2008.
39　Charles Baudelaire, 'The Painter of Modern Life', excerpted in *Art in Theory*, 496.
40　Walter Benjamin, *Charles Baudelaire: A Lyric Poet in the Era of High Capitalism* (London: New Left Books, 1973).
41　www.iwm.org.uk/blog/research/2015/06/when-the-fireweed-flowers (retrieved 24 February 2023).
42　As explained by Dr Michael Hartshorne, emeritus trustee of the National Museum of Nuclear Science and History in Albuquerque, New Mexico. https://www.livescience.com/nuclear-bomb-wwii-shadows.html (accessed 22 March 2023).
43　The artist in conversation with Mariko Finch for *Tate Etc*, Issue 32, 10 December 2014.
44　'How Ukrainian photographers captured a year of conflict', *FT magazine*, 17 February 2023.
45　In a short text describing the work on the artist's website, https://dimatolkachov.cargo.site/new-grasses (retrieved 20 September 2023).
46　Ibid.
47　*De Materia Medica*.
48　William Coles, *The Art of Simpling: An Introduction to the Knowledge and Gathering of Plants* (London: Nathaniel Brook, 1656).
49　Bradley C. Bennett, 'Doctrine of Signatures: An Explanation of Medicinal Plant Discovery or Dissemination of Knowledge?', *Economic Botany* 61, no. 3 (2007): 246–255.
50　Ibid., see abstract.
51　Ibid., see abstract.
52　See the case studies at Pesticide Action Network UK: www.pan-uk.org.
53　Blaise Pascal and A. Krailsheimer, *Pensées* (Revised edition, London: Penguin Classics, 1995).

September

54　Walt Whitman, *Leaves of Grass* (London: Collins Classics, 2015), 66.
55　Damien M. Hicks et al., 'Food for Pollinators: Quantifying the Nectar and Pollen Resources of Urban Flower Meadows', *PLoS ONE* 11, no. 6 (24 June 2016): e0158117, https://doi.or10.1371/journal.pone.0158117.
56　Timothy Morton, *All Art Is Ecological*. This extract published in Penguin Green Ideas 3 (London: Penguin Books, 2021), 95.
57　Maggie Nelson, *Bluets* (2nd edition, Seattle: Wave Books, 2019), 4–5.
58　Rachel Cusk, *Second Place* (London: Faber & Faber, 2021), 13.
59　Roger Phillips, *Wild Flowers of Britain: Over a Thousand Species by Photographic Identification*, edited by Tom Wellsted (London: Pan Books, 1983).
60　Robert MacFarlane, introduction to Shepherd, *The Living Mountain* (2011).
61　'Ragwort Fact File'. Archived from the original on 14 May 2012. Retrieved 31 March 2012. Accessed 21 September 2023. From Buglife, the Invertebrate Conservation Trust.
62　Extracts from the 'Aesthetic Excursus' in the *Four Books of Human Proportion* are included in Jeffrey Ashcroft, 'Art in German: Artistic Statements by Albrecht Dürer', *Forum for Modern Language Studies* 48, no. 4 (1 October 2012): 376–88, https://doi.org/10.1093/fmls/cqs025. Texts themselves are from Hans Rupprich, *Dürer. Schriftlicher Nachlass* (Berlin: Deutscher Verein für Kunstwissenschaft, 1956).
63　Ibid.

NOTES

October
64 Eduardo Navarro and Michael Marder, 'Vegetal Transmutation', in *This Book Is a Plant: How to Grow, Learn and Radically Engage with the Natural World* (London: Profile Books / Wellcome Collection, 2022), 3

65 Shepherd, *The Living Mountain*, 105.

66 Stefano Mancuso and Alessandra Viola, *Brilliant Green: The Surprising History and Science of Plant Intelligence*, translated by Joan Benham; foreword by Michael Pollan (Washington DC: Island Press, 2015), 115.

67 John Josselyn, *New-Englands Rarities* (1672), quoted by Grigson in *The Englishman's Flora*, 334.

68 Mabey, *Weeds*, 50

69 Maria Thereza Alves, quoted in Sam Phillips, 'Meet Six Contemporary Avant-Gardeners', *RA Magazine*, accessed 13 August 2023, https://www.royalacademy.org.uk/article/modern-garden-contemporary-artist-gardeners

November
70 Sean Borodale, *Bee Journal* (London: Jonathan Cape, 2012), 115.

71 Nancy Spero, 'Tracing Ana Mendieta', *ARTFORUM* 30, no. 8 (April 1992), https://www.artforum.com/print/199204/tracing-ana-mendieta-33595. Accessed 30 April 2022.

72 Psalm 103, 15–16.

73 Simryn Gill during an online talk at The Drawing Room, London, on 3 May 2022. Accessed 30 June 2023. https://drawingroom.org.uk/resources/drawing-room-at-20-artists-reflections-mark-dion-simryn-gill

74 Ibid.

December
75 Annie Dillard, Pilgrim at Tinker Creek (Norwich: Canterbury Press, 2011), p.270

76 John Keats to George and Thomas Keats, December 1817, in *Selected Letters*, edited by John Barnard (London: Penguin Classics, 2014).

77 Donald Barthelme, 'Not-Knowing' in Donald Barthelme and John Barth, *Not-Knowing: The Essays and Interviews of Donald Barthelme*, edited by Kim Herzinger (New York: Random House, 1997).

78 Alberto Giacometti and Angel González, *Alberto Giacometti: Works, Writings, Interviews* (Barcelona: Ed. Polígrafa, 2006), 141–142.

79 Mabey, *Weeds*, 289.

80 Rachel Hahn, 'Precious Okoyomon: An Interview on Growth, Death, and Forests', *Pin-Up*. Accessed 1 July 2023. https://pinupmagazine.org/articles/rachel-hahn-precious-okoyomon-interview

81 Georges Perec, 'The Street', in *Species of Spaces and Other Pieces* (London: Penguin, 1999), 50.

82 Adam Phillips, 'On Being Bored', in *On Kissing, Tickling and Being Bored: Psychoanalytic Essays on the Unexamined Life* (London: Faber and Faber, 1993), 75.

Postscript
83 Shepherd, *The Living Mountain*, 59.

ABOUT THE AUTHOR

Anna Chapman Parker is an artist, writer and teacher whose work explores relationships between drawing, writing, body and place. Her exhibitions and commissions include projects for Edinburgh Art Festival, The University of Glasgow, Cample Line and Commonroom.co. She has taught drawing at The Royal College of Art, The Futures Institute and in weedy carparks. Her writing has appeared in journals from *MAP* and *Happy Hypocrite* to *Resurgence & Ecologist*. *Understorey* is her first book.

Anna studied at The University of Edinburgh and The University of Arts, London. She lives in Northumberland.

annachapman.co.uk